The Agility Dog International

PETER LEWIS

Illustrations:

Training Photographs:
Eddie Gee

Courses:
Peter Lewis

Obstacles:
Alan Clubley

Dog Sketches by courtesy of
Sveriges Hundungdom
(Youth Organisation of the
Swedish Kennel Club)

CANINE PUBLICATIONS

CANINE PUBLICATIONS
21 Burridge Road, Burridge, Southampton SO3 7BY England
Telephone 0489 885112

THE AGILITY DOG

First Published   1981
Second Impression   1985

Totally revised to become:

THE AGILITY DOG INTERNATIONAL

ISBN 0 906422 08 6

Printed and bound in Great Britain by
A. Wheaton & Co. Ltd, Exeter
Typeset by Pacesetter, Portsmouth in 10/12 point Times Roman

Contents

Illustrations

Illustrations

In the Text

Foreword

The first ten years of Agility have seen an enormous growth in the number of participants and Agility events throughout the length and breadth of Great Britain, and more recently across Europe and many parts of the Western World.

The obstacles used for Agility today have not significantly changed since Peter Meanwell first introduced them to the public in 1978. The only additions being the Wishing Well and Crossover. The fact that there has been little change is testimony to the thought and knowledge originally applied by Peter and his friends from Lincoln.

During these ten years the standard of both dogs and handlers has greatly improved, but perhaps the most improvement has been in course design and judging. Many people have played their part in evolving these improvements but none more so than the author of this book Peter Lewis. Apart from being one of the country's leading competitors, Peter has worked tirelessly to improve dog safety, better training and instructing methods, and the highest standards of judging, using all his previously gained knowledge and experience from Working Trials and Obedience.

This book "The Agility Dog International" is a must for any potential enthusiast because of the Authors ability to start at the beginning with basics and, whilst still commanding interest, take the reader step by step through to the end in a clear and easy to understand way. It also makes excellent reading for the more experienced Agility handler, delving into much greater detail on training methods and problem solving than the original "Agility Dog". The chapter on Obstacle Design & Build is in itself worth the cost of the book. How many times has the club carpenter been asked to make equipment from a verbal description only to find when finished that it does not comply with regulations.

It is estimated that thousands of people are competing in Agility at the present time with many more enjoying the sport at club level. One thing is certain, all of these people will benefit from good sound advice based upon a wealth of knowledge. In this book they will get this and much much more.

John Gilbert.

1

About Agility

Agility Tests are a comparatively new form of dog competition where the animal's fitness and the handlers's ability to train and direct the dog over and through certain obstacles is tested. Whilst the basis of the sport is jumping hurdles no higher than 2′ 6″ the full set of Kennel Club approved equipment requires the dog to be agile in various ways. The 'A' Ramp being just over 6′ high with ramps on either side at roughly 45 degrees is an obstacle for the dog to scramble up and down. Another intriguing obstacle is the dog walk, so called because it would be a little peculiar to call it a cat walk. This has long ramps at either end with a 12′ long plank spanning the middle 4′ 6″ above the ground. Not only does it require a dog trained to be sure footed when walking at height on a narrow board but also tests his confidence. Requiring even greater confidence is the see-saw, which although also constructed with a narrow board but looking less imposing than the walk, is more difficult for the dog to master. He has a natural distrust of anything that is unsteady and will need to be taught how to master the tipping motion so that it holds no fear. A hoop, usually a tyre, suspended from a frame requires the dog to exercise great judgement to time his leap correctly if he is to safely pass through the narrow aperture. Two types of tunnel form part of the basic equipment. One is a semi-rigid tunnel that can be bent into various shapes such as a letter S. This is often used in conjunction with the 'A' Ramp so that having traversed the 'A' Ramp placed over the tunnel, the dog returns through the tunnel's bends to exit in the opposite direction. A canvas tunnel is also used. This usually has a rigid opening which allows the dog to enter before pushing his way through the canvas. Spectators love to watch the moving hump of the dog as he passes through. A long jump can be included as can a water jump which might prove tempting for the water loving dog. To test whether the dog is steady and under basic control a mandatory five second pause is required on a small table. As an alternative pause sometimes a 4' square described as a white outline will be placed upon the ground.

Perhaps the most difficult equipment for the dog to master is the weaving poles. Usually spaced 18" apart they consist of a number of poles through which the dog must weave or slalom.

All or some of these obstacles can be arranged into a course by a skilful judge who will ensure that handling skill plays as big a part as speed. In fact cleverly designed courses may require degrees of handling skill that if successful cancel out any advantage of sheer youth and speed. The majority of winners so far have been middle aged, proving Agility places a far higher premium upon training and handling skill than it does upon the handlers youth. That is not to say that handler fitness is unnecessary for obviously a skilful fit handler is likely to be the best combination.

Agility Tests are run against the clock which is necessary to ensure that handlers do not take their dogs round the course at a walking pace in the hope of ensuring a clear round. While the clock must play its part, like Show Jumping the main method of arriving at a result is for faults to be deducted when obstacles fall or are run past by the dog. However some Agility equipment cannot be knocked over so there are other ways of faulting the dog that does not traverse them correctly. This happens on the obstacles the dogs walk on for at both ends there are coloured areas with which the dog must make contact . It is not really a question of finding a way to fault the dog, but ensuring that the dogs are taught to walk all the way rather than jump off from a height. This is an important factor deliberately used in this sport to ensure that dogs do not continually land from heights that could eventually produce shoulder damage.

One of the sports greatest assets is that, providing basic obedience has already been acquired, good dogs and handlers correctly taught can obtain competition standard quickly. This means that there is no time for the dog to become bored with constant repetitive work which might have the effect of lowering the tail. Certainly the vast majority of dogs thoroughly enjoy the game that it is and the very small minority who are not keen are quickly retired. Even dogs that have already become bored with other forms of training readily display their willingness to take part in such a fun event. That small minority who show no enthusiasm are usually the type of dogs who are either naturally lethargic or who have been given a good reason to dislike jumping. Such a reason will either have been brought about by the handler or by the dogs health and fitness.

Any person of intelligent age can train and take part in Agility Tests with such a statement applying to young and old alike. Of course certain basic degrees of handler fitness are necessary so that mobility can be maintained. Many existing enthusiasts are looking forward to the day when through such skilled training it will be almost unnecessary for the handler to move. This is not difficult for a skilled trainer with the advantage of at least one practise round on a simple course. Where it becomes tricky is when competing on a course totally unfamiliar to the dog. However, with complex courses I doubt if it will be achievable in the future.

Sooner or later the question arises of what dogs are considered suitable for Agility Tests. There is no set answer to such a question other than to suggest that any dog of sufficient size and fitness to traverse all the regulation obstacles is a suitable prospect. Of course this is a deliberate over simplification, for some dogs smaller than average sized Shelties have been successful as have many large breeds such as German Shepherd dogs. Bearing in mind two breeds as diverse in build and conformation as these the reader can easily understand that within reason any build is suitable. To suggest as some might do, that smaller sized equipment should be made available for the toy breeds is not the answer. We already have Mini Classes for dogs not exceeding 15″ at the shoulder and once the hurdle heights are reduced to 15″ they are able to traverse all the standard equipment except the table. In this case a pause box is the ideal substitute. In my opinion the existing regulations regarding the size of obstacles allow for very many breeds to participate. The very fact that the courses being set by the judges require good degrees of skilled handling means that breeds slower by nature also have a chance to compete with their faster brothers. Without doubt there is not a lot wrong with the minimum and maximum obstacle sizes. If the reader feels that their particular breed is incapable of negotiating such sizes then perhaps the answer is to change breed.

The basic principles were all very carefully thought out by Peter Meanwell from Lincoln. Certainly it was improved upon when trials were conducted with a group of friends, but without Peter it is highly unlikely that the sport would exist today.

It all started during the latter half of 1977 when Peter was approached by John Varley, a member of the Crufts Dog Show Committee. John's responsibility was the spare time in the main arena between the end of the obedience championships and the commencement of the group breed judging. Various dog training demonstrations had been held over the years, some of which included dogs jumping. John Varley's idea was a dog jumping competition which probably owes its birth to his connection with the horse world. Being an excellent showman he knew the type of event he had in mind but needed a practical dog training person to supply the answers. He contacted Peter asking him to devise a test and the appropriate equipment, with part of the brief being that it should be suited to the hard Olympia floor. Peter's vast practical dog training knowledge plus many years spent as a successful Working Trials competitor and judge soon enabled him to plan the basic principle. The main factors he always kept in mind were that it should be a fun event without being dangerous and that it would provide spectator appeal.

Several of Peter's friends in the Lincoln area, who were to become his team members, helped build the equipment. He realised that to add interest it would be necessary to involve another club so he contacted Trevor Jones of the Yorkshire Working Trials Training Society to produce a team of four dogs. All the people involved at this stage helped each other with training ideas and modifications to equipment where it was felt that an improvement could be made. Eventually the two teams of four dogs plus one reserve arrived at Crufts Dog Show in February 1978 and the handlers changed into smart tracksuits as a team uniform. They competed against each other with such success that it was obvious from the crowd reaction that this innovation would be seen again. The following year of 1979, after qualifying rounds, three teams appeared, and these were the Pontefract Dog Training Club, The Rugby Dog Training Club and The Yorkshire Working Trials Society. A further Agility milestone was reached when the finals of a major competition were held at the International Horse Show at Olympia during December 1979. This was won by Mr Phil Cusworth's Border Collie, Canny Cluff, with an exciting final run that had the crowd roaring. John Varley had organised the event in conjunction with the Show Jumping officials and the sponsors.

The equipment used mainly consisted of hurdles plus the hoop, weaving poles and pause box, so that the event would simulate as near as possible a horse show jumping competition.

During 1979 the Kennel Club introduced regulations for Agility Tests and by doing so Agility was given official blessing. Up until the introduction of rules the sport had taken place on an unofficial basis, but clearly some governing legislation was to become necessary. Without it neither competitors, judges nor officials would have recourse to the governing body if problems or disputes arose. To make this possible, and for everyone involved to be acting within Kennel Club regulations, there had to be a system of granting licences. Obviously while this was being done it made sense for the Kennel Club to apply other basic rules such as the method of scoring and the approval of equipment. This latter point being most important, for the sport in its infancy had just a few knowledgeable dog people working together. Once its popularity had been established and in the absence of regulations anybody could invent an obstacle which might possibly prove to be injurious to the dog. Misguided enthusiasts might have decided to run a puissance competition where a jump or jumps become progressively higher or longer. There are those who question such events as run in Show Jumping competitions, saying that it is cruel and dangerous to the horse. Having no knowledge of horses or show jumping means that I have no right to express an opinion on this point. What I do know is that to have such a competition in canine agility events would be terribly dangerous for the dogs taking part and would inevitably produce a large crop of critics for the sport. There are some who feel that the maximum hurdle height of 2' 6" is much too low, suggesting that it should be at least 3' 6". I have owned a dog who easily cleared 4' but resisted the temptation to join the lobby for higher hurdles. This really is the point, for those with dogs who can master higher hurdles are the very people that want them raised. 2' 6" is sensible, it is not dangerous and allows many smaller dogs to compete. All things being considered, the Kennel Club rules take account of safety, and being worded simply they are easily understood. There is a lot to be said for simple regulations which allow freedom of action within the actual wording. A new regulation will often require further legislation to qualify the original. Hopefully Agility will avoid this trap that has so beset Obedience Dog Shows in Great Britain.

The first Agility Test to be run under the new Kennel Club

regulations was the event staged at Crufts 1980. The three teams to qualify at an eliminating round to compete at this event were The Pontefract Dog Training Club, The Yorkshire Working Trials Training Society and the Waldridge Fell Dog Training Club. Appropriately it was judged by Peter Meanwell, who having been mainly responsible for the sports development, had the onerous task of being the first judge to interpret the regulations. Without doubt this was a wise choice, for who could be better than the sports innovator to handle the first official test. Knowing my enthusiasm he had asked me to act as his score steward which I willingly accepted as I wished to play a full role in helping to establish what he had started. In the very brief time we were in the main Crufts arena it was apparent that this sport was a winner with the spectators. The reaction of the crowd being so generous made it obvious that the Kennel Club had, for the first time, a genuine spectator sport on their hands. All the ingredients of crowd appeal were apparent. Each dog completed a round in under one minute so no spectator had to concentrate on a particular dog for long periods of time. The way a dog was faulted, whilst inevitably not being quite so simple as Show Jumping, was so much easier for the spectator to understand than other forms of dog competition. The fact that the dogs competed against the clock injected a speed element and with all these facts thrown together the result was an all action event that pleased the crowds. All these points plus the fact that the wagging tails indicated a high measure of canine enjoyment told me that this now official dog sport would not die.

Following Crufts 1980 and the growing realisation that it was unlikely Crufts 1981 would stage Agility Tests, the North of England being the originators of the event lost a certain amount of enthusiasm. This was more than countered by the South of England awakening to the challenge of Agility. Several Southern training classes started operating on a more regular basis, quickly learning the best methods of teaching newcomers.

Dog training competitions have traditionally relied on many unsung heroes who work ceaselessly without seeking recognition of any kind. The South during 1980 produced such a person who had built all the equipment and was prepared to transport and erect it for various competitions. Ted Groome played a great part in establishing Agility in the South of England. Very soon he realised that being a spectator sport, public address systems and digital public timing readouts would make for far greater interest and he worked ceaselessly towards this end until his premature death in 1984.

During the winter of 1980/81 Agility training by Ted and myself continued indoors at the Calshot Activities Centre on the Southampton outskirts so that their handlers would be well prepared for the 1981 season. However prior to this during 1980 several Agility Tests were successfully held culminating with the semi-finals of the main competition being held at Stoneleigh, Warwickshire. This event was to provide the final 20 dogs for the major event at the International Horse Show at Olympia 1980, and the South for the first time at any national competition almost provided fifty per cent of the competitors to go forward to the final. My own 10 year old Border Collie, Spot, was a finalist and indeed won his Olympia heat. However the eventual winner was Les Robinson of Haslemere, Surrey with his Border Collie bitch, Homestead Good Luck Charm. Les had two very fast clear rounds on the final day to make him the winner against the clock. So the sport that had originated in the North had truly become national, for now the South had produced a major winner to enable the doors of Agility to open across the length of the country.

In its original form Agility consisted of one standard event over a course designed in a figure of eight with a table at the centre on which the dog was expected to pause for five seconds. Such a one class system usually allowed for the competitors to run twice over the course, counting the best of the two runs or both being added together. The fact that each dog was allowed to run twice often gave rise to problems, particularly where only one of the two rounds counted. A crafty handler could use the first round as a very slow practise to show the dog the route, then go flat out at the second attempt. It became obvious that the best system was one attempt only which gave the ability to handle with skill a further impetus. The only snag was that such a system meant that the handlers may well have travelled many miles to be in the ring for less than one minute which hardly seemed worthwhile. The logical progression was for a system of classes to develop that would ensure every dog would be able to be entered in a minimum of two classes. In its first year as a Kennel Club recognised sport, it became quite obvious that the prizes would usually be shared amongst a minority of superior dogs with the 'also rans' having little or no chance. Whilst no one wanted to see a system develop whereby many classes must be worked through to reach the top, the solution was to provide one or two classes from which the better dogs were excluded. The experiments in this direction proved successful during 1980, and then in 1981 we saw the first introduction of novelty classes which would also require a high degree of skilled dog handling. Mrs. C. C. Guard scheduled a Gamblers Stake at the Haslemere Dog Training Club's Agility Test which proved to be very effective in terms of thought and skill. Being interested in snooker I had been very impressed with the Snooker Stakes in which the horses competed at Olympia, and easily adapted that competition to suit Agility. Later in this book the classification and novelty competitions are explained. When carefully put together a schedule of Agility can provide two or more classes for each dog in a day. Indeed sometimes there are too many classes but it is always the competitor who decides whether or not to enter every class.

In order to bring as many Agility enthusiasts together as possible, Peter Meanwell and I got together to formulate the idea of a North versus South match. It was obvious that this event would be best sited in the centre of the country, so we called in Ted Pallot of the Rugby Dog Training Club to organise the event. The match eventually took place during the summer of 1981 as part of a two day Agility weekend with 35 dogs in each team. The South were the winners of this historic event and were presented with a magnificent shield to be fought over annually. As Captain of the Southern team, ably assisted by John Gilbert, I was proud that the South had won the first encounter, but knew my Agility friends in the North would be out to reverse the result in 1982.

1981 also saw the major Agility event being scheduled with the full Kennel Club approved equipment. Mr. Norman Hills was the organiser on behalf of the sponsors, and the first two dogs of each 12 heats qualified to compete in December at the International Horse Show at Olympia. Roger Farr created history by qualifying three German Shepherd Dogs for the final, and I was pleased to qualify my Border Collie, Spot, again with the intention of retiring him at Olympia. I also qualified my young collie, Amos on Appro, affectionately known as Moss.

In November 1983 my good friend John Gilbert and I decided to see if the majority of competitors would be interested in a National Club. They overwhelmingly were for the sport had reached the stage where some kind of uniformity was desperately needed. This applied particularly to the class structure which was different at every show. The Club has prospered and is largely responsible for the uniformity and order that prevails today. They also involve themselves in the safety of equipment, with handling and judging courses also regularly undertaken across the country. The Club's monthly journal, The Agility Voice, is a must for the intending competitor and is in fact read in many countries of the world. I am very proud to have been associated with it and can only heap praise on the responsible committee with whom it has been my privilege to work.

I have had a lot of fun with Agility, indeed its growth across the world has enabled me to visit many other countries to teach and judge. Even when there are language barriers, talking to doggy people is not that difficult. Agility is without doubt one of the best things to have happened to the dog competition world, what is strange is why it took so long coming.

2

Control of the Dog

To be able to teach a dog to jump on command is reasonably easy providing that it is taught in a manner that will give the dog confidence. To be able to teach a dog to jump on command and maintain complete control without lead assistance requires a skilled dog trainer. While a certain amount of jumping training can be carried out before the handler has the control, a well trained dog will learn his new job more quickly. Such a statement poses the question of what constitutes a well trained dog. For me the answer is a dog that will respond on one command when he is called, when told to sit, wait, walk to heel and go down. I stress one command because there is a world of difference between a dog that requires repetitive commands and the one that obeys instantly. To be able to stand in front of a 2′ 6″ hurdle with the dog sitting quietly at heel without the lead attached, give one command to which the dog will jump and give a further command which will keep the dog stationary on the far side, is a demonstration of controlled jumping. Far better that the control has been taught prior to Agility lessons for the dog then has less to learn, less to misunderstand and any compulsion necessary for control will not be associated with Agility. The novice reader may ask why control compulsion should not have an Agility association, and the answer is that jumping itself requires certain degrees of compulsion. Dogs differ widely in their nature and while some harder dogs will accept a lot of compulsion, a softer dog will not. All that will happen is that it will go to pieces, put it's tail down and cease to enjoy jumping. This is exactly the opposite to the effect to be achieved, for Agility should be a fun event, not only for the handler, but primarily for the dog.

The point that I shall stress several times throughout this book is that the training aim should at all times be to give the dog confidence. A dog that has this will learn very quickly and display his enjoyment by wagging his tail. Having established that good control is a great asset some explanation of how it can be achieved becomes necessary.

THE RECALL

Competing and training for Agility means that the dog will often be running free. Many temptations may distract him or the course may be better completed using partial recalls at various times. Certainly without the ability to call the dog back instantly, training and competing should not be attempted. The best place to learn this is at the local dog training club because at such an establishment the dog will learn to come when called even though he is in the company of other dogs.

Those readers who are about to buy a puppy can make life very easy for themselves and the dog by teaching the natural recall method at each feeding time. The puppy will need to be fed several times during the day and each meal can be used as the basis of a recall. Having prepared the food, make an interesting shooshing or whispering sound that gains the puppy's attention. As he reaches you, place the food dish on the ground by your feet and praise him. The puppy's name should be used between the interesting sound, and gradually the command 'Come' can be interspersed until just the puppy's name and command are all that are necessary. Such education is not really training, and if correctly undertaken will make a more compulsive method obsolete. Unfortunately not everyone is sufficiently enlightened about training at the time they purchase their dog, and very often the dog will have become an adult without learning to 'come when called'. If the reader has such a dog then the following procedure can be adopted.

It is preferable for the dog to wear a check chain or training collar (incorrectly referred to as a choke). The chain should be large enough to avoid a struggle to fit on the dog, but when pulled tight should not have more than 3″ to 4″ spare. There are two ways the collar can be worn and only one is correct. The incorrect way will mean that the collar will act as a choke which, whilst being somewhat cruel, is also completely useless for training. To ensure that this does not happen the links of the chain should be allowed to drop through one of the two large rings found at each end of the chain. The handler, facing the dog, should hold the threaded chain so that it forms a figure '6' lying on its front, with the loop of the '6' in the right hand and the spare chain in the left. It can now be slipped over the dog's head to form a training collar with the ring that the links run through on the left side of the dog's neck. The collar, correctly worn, will tighten when the handler zips the lead and slacken as soon as the zip is completed. With the lead attached at the end of the chain's tail it will be possible to correct the dog by a quick zip of the lead.

Having ensured that the collar is worn correctly, attach a good strong lead made either of traditional bridle leather, nylon or webbing. It should be 3' to 4' long with a strongly stitched handle and a good quality trigger hook. To make it possible to teach the recall the dog must first be taught to sit. Holding the lead gently pulled tight by the right hand above his head, the left hand should push the dog's hindquarters into the sit position simultaneously giving the command 'Sit'. This is a compulsive movement which should be achieved upon the one command for the handler has complete control of the dog with the lead and free hand. Immediately the dog sits praise should be given so that he knows that he has done well, but the handler must guard against excessive praise that may make him excited enough to move. Traditionally the heel position has been the left side of the handler and during any competition heelwork the dog will be required to work on this side. It therefore makes sense that tradition should be followed even though the handler may not have ideas of working in competitions other than Agility. However should the reader wish to take part in Obedience or Working Trials it is advisable that the dog is placed in a straight heel sit at each first attempt. Failure to do so will teach the dog to sit crooked with a possible loss of marks each time he does so. If Agility is to be the sole aim of the handler then the angle the dog sits at is quite immaterial.

Having taught the dog to sit, give the command 'Wait', then using the right foot step slightly to the side away from him. Whilst doing so hold the lead in the right hand but allow it to run over the left hand just above the dog's head making it tight so that he cannot move. Stepping to the side with the right foot avoids confusion with heelwork training where always stepping forward with the left foot will become a signal for the dog to move off with the handler. When leaving the dog to subsequently call him, the sideways step with the right foot should always be used, but in this case the handler is going to stand in front of the dog with the lead held taut. After a few such lessons if he is not attempting to move the lead can be slackened but the left hand should remain in the same position to re-apply the tension if necessary.

Once the dog has learned to sit and remain steady in this position the handler can slowly back off to the end of a slack lead, gently praising the dog but returning to correct immediately should he move. One of the secrets of keeping the dog steady while backing away is to ensure that at no time does the lead tighten, if it does it will only induce him to move. With the dog sitting steady at the end of a slack lead held with the right hand through the handle and the left hand immediately below, the handler is ready to proceed. Giving the lead a quick zip so that both hands finish in the groin should have the effect of encouraging the dog towards the handler. At the same time the dogs name and the command 'Come' should be given followed by praise if his response warrants it. As he arrives in front the handler can quickly lean forward and tap his backside with the hand whilst saying 'Sit'. The tap must not be overdone for the dog could form the habit of sitting well away to avoid it. This training sequence for the recall should be repeated several times during a training session, but all dog training can be overdone so little and often is the best motto.

A dog is a creature of habit and quickly learns a sequence of events which often he will attempt to anticipate. The wary dog handler must therefore guard against anticipation of the next step in any training sequence, and having backed away from the dog it is likely that he will try to come before the command and lead movement are used. Any attempted anticipation during dog training must not go unchecked, and in this case if the dog anticipates the handler must immediately return to his side and start again. If anticipation is tolerated it will not cure itself but rather become worse each time the dog gets away with it.

THE IMMEDIATE DOWN

One piece of Agility equipment that is sometimes used is the pause box. Generally it is a white square of 4' in which the dog is required to stay down for a five second pause. In dog training language we use the term 'Immediate Down' to denote exactly what it says – a dog who will drop immediately on one command. The pause box should hold no fear as a good trainer will have already mastered the immediate down for domestic purposes and will only need to give the command when the dog is over the box. A dog who can be dropped instantly is less likely to cause any type of accident providing the handler is aware of a problem and in a position to command 'Down'. Therefore it must be accepted as an essential part of dog training.

The ability to drop the dog instantly at a distance is the end product, but before that the handler must teach the dog to go down on the lead. This is probably the most compulsive training the dog will have to undergo and therefore it should be realised that he may struggle against the attempts to get him into the down position. The handler must be firm, not giving way in sympathy to the dog's struggles or complaints, for it is in his interests that he learns to respond immediately. With the dog sitting in the heel position hold the lead handle in the right hand, with the left hand loosely on the lead at the top next to the handle. Quickly slide the left hand down the lead until it reaches the training collar, and as it does so compel the dog to the floor giving the command 'Down' in an authoritative manner. As the dog goes down the handler will find it easier if he drops onto the left knee, and this will also avoid bending over the dog which is not good practise. Usually the dog will struggle, but once he has ceased doing so the handler can use the left foot on the lead to hold the dog down, thus freeing the left hand to fondle him while he is being praised. If the dog is not attempting to rise the handler can stand up, continuing the praise while doing so. Compelling the dog to the floor in this way will have to be repeated several times over several training sessions, but occasionally the pressure applied to the lead by the left hand can be slackened to give the dog the chance to go down without assistance. When this happens the dog is getting the idea and should be praised, but it may still be necessary to revert to compulsion if he does not respond immediately. Remember that if during training a second command is necessary it must be accompanied by compulsion, for during Agility competitions against the clock slow reactions cost time. However far more important is the ability to be able to drop the dog at any time, for the owner that is unable to do so does not have a trained dog.

Once the dog is responding on his own accord the handler can gradually move away, still retaining a degree of control by keeping the left foot on the lead. In due course the movement the left hand has been making will be recognised by the dog as a signal, and this combined with the command, will be sufficient without using any compulsion whatsoever.

Until the dog will go down by the handlers side the instant the command is given and without the aid of a hand signal, no attempt should be made to drop him at a distance. When attempting to do so, the further away he is from his handler the less submissive he will become, so care must be taken to ensure that there is a gradual lengthening of distance between handler and dog. One way this can be achieved is by running with the dog attached to the lead giving the command 'Down' and ensuring that obedience is instant by the use of the lead and the left hand. Gradually it will be possible for this manoeuvre to be carried out with the dog responding a full leads length away, but too much repetition in any one session will make a clever dog likely to anticipate. If this does happen intersperse occasions when the handler runs without attempting to drop him. A dog will very quickly learn a sequence of events which can be an advantage at some times and a disadvantage at others.

When over several training sessions the dog has always obeyed instantly at the full length of the lead, the immediate down can be attempted without it. Once the dog is aware that the lead is not attached he may not respond to the command because he thinks he is no longer under control. It therefore makes sense for the first attempts at lead-free to be carried out with the dog beside the handler, only moving away to drop him as progress is made. Little by little over a period of time the distance from the dog can be increased. The handler however must remember that if at a distance a second or more command is necessary, reversion to the previous stage of training is imperative to ensure instant obedience. Progression can be made again later but there can be no short cuts, and perfection will probably only be achieved after weeks of patient build-up.

HEELWORK

The reader may ask where heelwork is used during an Agility competition, the answer being that it can have many uses. In the first place the handler will have to walk out into the arena with the dog on a lead. Walking with a dog under close control is really the act of heelwork and the ability to arrive at the starting point in a calm and professional manner will be of benefit to handler and dog. During a round there can be many occasions where the handler wishes to call the dog to heel, even using fast heelwork from one jump to another while negotiating a tricky part of the course. It therefore becomes apparent that the ability to hold the dog at heel on one command can be a great advantage.

To teach heelwork the dog should be wearing a training collar, a good lead and be sitting quietly in the heel position. The handler must understand the correct starting sequence based on the numbers '1, 2, 3'. '1' being the dogs name to gain his attention, '2' being the command 'Heel', followed by '3', the act of stepping off and moving the left foot forward. The reader will remember that when leaving the dog for a recall the right foot should be moved first. Moving the left foot for heelwork helps to avoid confusion between the two exercises, and being the nearest leg to the dog has the added bonus of drawing him forward. The lead and its excess should be held in the right hand allowing approximately 9″ of slack looped across the body. The handler can move off in a straight line, or preferably large slow left-hand circles, using the '1, 2, 3' sequence in the space of a second. Should the dog attempt to move ahead, the command 'Heel' must be repeated while gently running the left hand down the lead to ease him back into the correct position. Should he be the type of dog that after several attempts will not respond to such gentle treatment, allow him to get to the end of the lead momentarily releasing the tension to be able to give a hard sharp lead check while simultaneously using the command 'Heel'. If correctly carried out the collar tension will slacken immediately after the check has been given, and this is the moment for the dog to be praised. One such correction may be sufficient, or with an older dog that has always been allowed to pull on the lead, to make him desist, many such corrections may be necessary.

It is possible that a young dog unused to the lead and training collar will put his behind on the ground and refuse to move, in the hope that such action will end the training session. With such a case the handler should walk to the end of the lead and when resistance is felt, continue to walk in the same manner. This will have the effect of either forcing him to his feet or being dragged in the sitting position. The likely outcome is that after a few yards he will get to his feet and that will be the signal for the handler to encourage him to the heel position. In such a way it has been demonstrated that it is far more comfortable to walk than be dragged.

At this stage it is extremely unlikely that the dog will start lagging as this is usually the result of constant unnecessary nagging by a handler who has misunderstood the use and timing of the lead. With such a case the dog will associate the command 'Heel' with unpleasantness, the lead with apprehension, and the handler with suspicion. Curing lagging is almost impossible. Certainly the lead should rarely correct, and having done the damage must never nag again. Instead any successful method of encouraging the dog to walk at heel should be substituted.

If all goes well the left-hand circle can now become more oblong, which will have the effect of making the bends left wheels. At this stage the handler should walk in a manner that bends slightly from side to side as though carrying out an exaggerated weave. This will be a series of left and right wheels which can slowly be changed into full turns. Although having started training in left-hand circles it is probably better to first turn the right wheel into a full right turn. This can soon be followed by the about turn which is only an extension of the former turn. Should the dog attempt to go wide with any of these turns the handler must immediately zip the lead accompanied by the command 'Heel' and followed with praise if the dog responds as expected.

During all heelwork training it is totally unnecessary to bend over the dog, it being far more preferable to maintain an upright posture. The temptation to bend and watch the dog will be there, but with diligence it can be avoided.

To train a dog to walk perfectly at heel without the assistance of the lead is really quite simple. If the previous advice has been faithfully and correctly followed then the dog will be ready for the lead to be removed without any noticeable difference in the standard of his heelwork. Certainly he may require more encouragement to be held in the heel position, but if that is insufficient the handler must revert to lead heelwork training.

Heelwork at the fast pace will probably prove to be the most useful for the Agility dog. When first teaching the fast pace the handler should perfect it as straight lines before progressing to turns and without any halts, for it is very easy to collide with the dog whilst both are learning to work together at speed. Such collisions will only confuse him, so perfect straight lines first before gently introducing turns at the fast pace.

As heelwork sits play no part in Agility no mention has been made of them. The over-use of the heelwork sit can be a contributory cause to general apprehension with its associated lagging, and as the sport to be pursued should be great fun for dog and handler, lagging and apprehension have no place. Likewise only the basic exercises necessary for Agility control have been dealt with, for general obedience training can be read in other books.

The next part of this chapter deals with more advanced Obedience, but all that has been read so far, if put into practise will be sufficient to enable the commencement of obstacle training.

SENDAWAY

A good fast accurate sendaway is a great asset to the Agility dog. It should be obvious that whilst competing, the ability to send the dog on ahead would be a great advantage. Indeed many handlers do so particularly over the last two hurdles and away to the finish. What may not be quite so obvious is that a sendaway can be quickly converted to teach the dog a fast and spectacular weave without the handler being beside the dog. This is dealt with in Chapter 3 where the method of teaching each obstacle is detailed.

For the purpose of Agility the sendaway needs to be split into two categories. Training to a box as is sometimes taught for Obedience shows, and training the dog to run on ahead more as he would be required to do at a Working Trial. While the sendaway in these two sports does not require speed of the dogs movement, in Agility Tests it becomes a great advantage for the dog to have sendaway speed. For this reason it should be obvious to the reader that the sendaway command should not be connected with apprehension by the dog, for if so his reaction is likely to be reluctant slow obedience. Every effort must be made during training to avoid any suspicion of duress, which once again becomes far easier to avoid if the basic training has been mastered. The handler has to be able to control the dog at the end of a sendaway, with the logical way to do so being to drop the dog in the down position as already discussed. Even if the dog initially associates immediate down training with duress it does not matter too much as long as the response is instantaneous. What must not happen is for the dog to associate any duress with the sendaway, so therefore sendaway and immediate down training must not be combined until the latter has been perfected and the dog will instantly drop at a distance when required to do so. This also means that the dog must not associate the pause box with apprehension for it is to the handlers advantage to be able to send him forward to this piece of equipment. It cannot be overstressed that down training should not be carried out in a pause box nor should it have any training association with the sendaway. It is taught separately as a basic, and when and only when thoroughly learned, added as a component part of advanced control.

The finest method I know of teaching the sendaway is to do so when the dog is a puppy. Because he will most likely still be a little ball of fluff, I use the word teaching quite deliberately for it will be a case of educating him rather than formal training. It can and should be taught long before the puppy wears his first training check chain, for such an aid has no part to play with this education. The sole aim will be to establish a series of repetitive situations which will always have a pleasurable association. In the chapter on basic training I suggested that a puppy could easily be trained for a recall by using his feeding times. Likewise the basis of a sendaway can be taught in his new home from the very first meal that he is given. If the handler has started recall training to the food dish, within forty eight hours the food dish can be substituted by recalls to hand held tit-bits, thus allowing his mealtimes to be used for sendaways.

The most suitable food dish for the purpose is the type that is finished in white enamel. As the puppy learns, it is preferable to be able to progressively reduce the size of the feeding dish which can be easily simulated by items such as tin lids painted white. Initially the white food dish will have a visual meaning for the puppy, but as his learning progresses and the dish becomes smaller he will rely more upon the commands. The first aim is to enable the puppy to associate the sendaway command with pleasure, so the chosen word should not have a harsh sound. Whilst the adult dog may need teaching in a manner that requires a strong word of command, the puppy is to learn by the association of pleasant ideas. Therefore an easy sound such as "Away" being a totally different sound to any other used with the dogs training to date, is most suitable for this purpose. To be avoided like the plague is the command "Go" which whilst probably sounding apt when spoken in the manner of a chief sending forth his braves, is too easily confused with "No". The associations the dog has with the word "No" will be exactly opposite to those that are to be achieved. Even dog owners who have never had any form of training instruction will have consistently used this word to convey their displeasure. The suggested command of "Away" can and should be used in a soft tone of voice without any necessity for the handler to shout, for the volume of the voice has little to do with successful dog training.

Having prepared the puppy's food in the white feeding dish it should be held in one hand while the puppy is tucked under the free arm. By ensuring that he can see the food and the fact that he is probably hungry, with luck he will be struggling to get to it. The handler should place the dish on the ground prior to backing away by two or three paces, while ensuring that the puppy does not lose sight of the dish. If correctly carried out his struggles to get to the food dish may even have intensified, so he should be gently lowered to the ground and quietly given the command "Away" as he is released. Thus the necessity to feed puppies several times a day becomes a great teaching advantage probably taking no extra time whatsoever. If this system is carried out at each meal time he will quickly learn to associate "Away" with pleasure, enabling him to grow up having learned to happily leave his handler on command. As he becomes older and thus bigger, it will no doubt become impossible to tuck the larger breed under the arm. By then he will be wearing a plain collar, so the handler having placed his food dish on the ground, can guide him with the lead to the place he is to start from. At this stage the distance between the starting point and the food dish should gradually have been lengthened by several yards and therefore more formal teaching can take over.

The pause box in the form of a 4' white painted square can be introduced, with the addition of markers such as upturned flower pots or pegs being placed on each of the four corners. The puppy attached to the lead should be taken to the box to see the food dish placed at the back almost touching the line. Obviously he must be made aware that food or tit-bits are in the dish or the absence of them will quickly bring the realisation that he is being fooled. Having been taught the command "Away" the idea of introducing the pause box is not just for him to associate the two things but also to be able to teach him to focus upon command. The puppy should now be taken to a starting point which playing safe will be half the distance he has so far been accustomed to. He should be placed in the heel position and if he has already learned to sit so much the better, but what he is about to be taught can be done while he stands providing that he is still. Using the hands to act like horse blinkers, the handler should place them either side of the puppies eyes, thus creating a narrow channel that allows him to see the box to the exclusion of any other side distraction. While this is being done the handler can quietly be repeating "Look straight" until sure that the puppy is looking at the box. When this is so and after maybe one more repetition of the words, the handler should say "Away" letting the puppy move through the hands so that he can run to the food dish. Being very compulsive it is unlikely that the down has been taught, so it should not be attempted when he reaches the box. Far better to let him eat whatever is in the dish having quietly and quickly accompanied him there ensuring that once the food has been eaten he does not run around. Later when the down has been thoroughly learned and its use combined with the sendaway, prior to being given the command "Down" he should be allowed to eat the tit-bit. Of course by this time the white dish will have been progressively substituted by smaller white markers containing the bait to which he is being lured. As the puppy learns, the distance should be increased by moving the starting point rather than the box, which for the initial stages should always remain in the same place. The corner markers of the box are there to enable the puppy to associate finish flags and timing devices with the commands, so that when in an Agility competition he can be easily sent on ahead to finish where necessary.

So far the teaching has been to send the puppy to the box, but long before the white feeding marker is dispensed with he must be taught to run through boxes rather than stop in them. If during training the puppy is always taught to stop at the box, there will come a time when anticipation takes over and he starts to prematurely hesitate before reaching it. This is overcome by teaching him to run through the box to his feeding marker which should be left progressively further on from the box. The reader may think this defeats the object, but at a later date running through boxes and the immediate down will be combined so that the dog can be dropped inside the box. The other reason is that the handler will also need to have the ability to get the dog in the heel position, and, getting him to focus on his food dish 50 to 100 yards away, the dog can be taught to "look straight" to virtually nothing. Of course from several yards to long distances will be a gradual progression. At a distance the dish will appear very small and later it can be substituted with a white stick prior to dispensing with markers altogether. Thus the dog is taught to "look straight" to boxes, markers, and to nothing, and this command will be associated with "Away" which will usually follow. At this stage it must be obvious that the handler should have the ability to control the dog immediately he has reached the designated point. To be continually shouting 'down' or 'stand still' at the end of a successful attempt is to risk confusion that he has incorrectly performed the sendaway, when in fact the end control is all that is wrong.

Earlier I mentioned the adult dog devoid of previous sendaway teaching. While the food dish method may partially work for some adult dogs it is less likely that he can be taught a reliable sendaway in this fashion. If the latter is the case, then the next step is to constantly recall the dog to the designated point prior to sending him there. This will take time and patience, but it is preferable to running with an awkward dog on a long slack lead repeating the chosen command. Of all sendaway methods this one has the least chance of teaching the dog accuracy, particularly if he is already lethargic with his training. When teaching the sendaway by the method described, if at any time the dog starts to veer off course it is preferable to call him back rather than let him continue in the wrong direction or give other commands that may confuse him. The instant the dog looks like going wrong, re-call him and on no account attempt to set him up to be sent again until action has been taken to ensure that the mistake is not repeated. If this is not done he will invariably make the same mistake, for a dogs natural instinct is to return to where he was previously going. To overcome this instinct the handler should leave the dog at the starting position and go to the place he had been focused to. This may be a pole, the feeding dish, box, or nothing, for it really does not matter. What does matter is re-calling him to the correct place and dropping him at the feet when he arrives. Following such evasive action the handler can set the dog up and send him again from a shorter distance than originally attempted. This time it is unlikely that the dog will repeat his mistake, and while the reader may think such actions fruitless, the great achievement has been that the dog has not been allowed to go wrong.

A further aid that will ensure the dog cannot go in the wrong direction is to take the opportunity of practising sendaways wherever a long straight narrow path is encountered. Such training is a must for those who wish to build confidence in the dog to keep going away even though the distance from the handler increases alarmingly. By sending the dog back the way that has just been walked he is not being sent somewhere that is unfamiliar. Also the point at which he is stopped can always remain the same, while the handler increases distance for the next attempt by walking further on. This path training has tremendous benefits for the Agility dog, as later on the handler can run behind him while continuing to send the dog forward by command. During Agility competitions the value of being able to send the dog on to anything, be it the next jump, marker poles, timing device, table or pause box, must give the handler of such a dog an advantage. Likewise if other dog training sports are also to be pursued, the sendaway teaching method I have described will be a sound basis for competition work.

DIRECTIONAL CONTROL

The ability to directionally control the Agility dog by voice and or signals is an aid to skilled handling and can save precious seconds in the competition ring. Hand signals alone are not sufficient for in many situations the dog will be working on ahead with a command only being suitable to turn him left or right. However hand signals definitely have their place when the dog can see them so a combination of the two is of most benefit.

Providing a few basic rules are observed re-direction is not as difficult as some think. The first rule is the one most handlers are tempted to break, for until the dog has thoroughly and independently mastered both the sendaway and directional control the two should never be trained in conjunction with one another. The next rule is during training sessions of any exercise the handler must be conscious of leg and arm movements. If not, the dog will easily become confused as to when he should or should not react to a signal. The last rule is just as important as the others in that the handler should perfect either right or left hand directional control, but never practice the two during the same session until the dog is thoroughly conversant with both.

Prior to directional control being attempted the handler must have the ability to stop the dog on one command at a distance in either the stand, sit or down position. Without such ability it is really impossible to teach this advanced training exercise, and attempting to do so will break all the rules of building upon basic training.

The ideal place to start is a field with a long wire fence, or failing this a similar kind of boundary can be set up in the garden. The draw back with the latter approach is that most gardens are too small for a long enough boundary to be created, as at least 100 yards or metres is necessary for effective training. When a suitable location has been established the dog should be placed on the opposite side of the fence, so that when the handler later moves back from the fence the dogs natural initial inclination to follow will be thwarted. At first approximately two or three yards should be the distance between dog and handler, who having given the chosen command and signal, should run alongside the fence repeating the command while keeping the signal arm raised. The dog will most likely naturally run with the handler, but if not he must be encouraged to do so. The obvious commands to use would be 'left' and 'right', although both ending with a hard pronounced letter 'T' have a similar sound to sit. If the sound of these two words is altered by accentuating the first part and almost making the 'T' silent, sufficient difference should have been created.

When running with the fence between dog and handler a good distance should be covered before stopping to praise him for his actions. Having done so the sequence can be repeated by commencing at the starting place again. On the first occasion probably four or five runs with the handler going all the way will be sufficient. On subsequent training sessions it must be gauged when to attempt to let him get ahead, so that eventually the handler can stand still with the dog reacting to the command and signal. At this point the handler should gradually drop back from the fence while the dog is running, for in this way the dog cannot see his handler move further away. As confidence is built the distance between dog, fence and handler can be increased, but initially at each session the dog should be given a full length redirection. Remember that only one direction is being taught, so the next progression is to commence the training session with a full length run which can be followed by dropping the dog half way before sending him on again. The reason that the full distance should be used at the start of each session is that if not the handler will find it difficult to send the dog beyond the point at which he is first stopped.

At all times concentrate on building the dogs confidence which naturally tends to diminish as the distance from his handler increases. Encouraging praise given at the right times will help considerably, but beware of unnecessary idle chatter which will only become an incessent drone to the dog. Once one direction has been perfected the opposite one can be taught in exactly the same way. However the handler should find a quicker response from the dog who is being asked to do exactly as he did before only in the opposite direction. The other changes come from the handler's use of a different arm and command.

Once both directions have been independently mastered they can be safely used consecutively. Whilst at this stage it would be technically possible to add the re-direction and sendaway together, to do so is best reserved for competition purposes. The danger of continually sending a dog away only to give him further directions is that he will start to take little interest in the direction in which he is initially being sent. The reason being that the constant repetitious change of directions may convince him that it matters not what he does first time, for he will be given further signals anyway.

3

Obstacle Training

When teaching jumping the first consideration must be the dog's fitness. Unless the handler is satisfied that the dog has no physical disabilities such as hip dysplasia, veterinary advice should be sought before training is attempted. Many owners over feed their dogs thinking that they are being kind when in fact all they achieve is to make them too fat. The result of carrying excessive weight probably shortens the dog's life which is not what the kind owner wishes to achieve. Before any serious jumping is attempted the owner should ensure that the dog is not overweight, dieting him and increasing his exercise if necessary.

British Kennel Club regulations for Agility Tests state "puppies under twelve calendar months of age are not eligible for competition". It should therefore go without saying that serious training should not be attempted until the dog has reached one year of age, and indeed with some of the slower maturing breeds one year is considered too young. If the handler has any doubt then I would suggest that they wait until the dog is 15 months of age, for most breeds bones have matured by then. There is, of course, nothing wrong in teaching a young dog jumping commands by taking him over a 9″ scaffold plank laid on its edge, providing that the temptation to progress to greater heights is resisted.

Unlike the vertical scale jump used in other forms of dog training competitions the Agility 'A' Ramp does not allow the dog to land from a 6′ height without penalty. The result is therefore an obstacle that is judged in a manner that requires safe negotiation by the dog.

The long jump is of the same design as that used for other competitions. However, where they require the long jump to be a maximum of 9′ long, during Agility competitions five feet length is more likely to be encountered.

A book such as this may teach the beginner handler many things but it is no substitute for good sound personal instruction. While equipment such as weaving poles and hurdles can be safely taught without supervision, I am of the opinion that the bigger pieces of equipment should only be taught to the dog and handler under expert instruction. For example when first being introduced to the equipment it is necessary for the dog to be on a collar and lead, and expert instruction can avoid handlers 'stringing their dogs up' by poor handling. My own rule is that when a handler is ready to move on to another piece of equipment they do so under instruction so that they can be shown the correct approach.

Most handlers will arrive for the first time with their dog wearing a check chain. This training aid is virtually irreplaceable for obedience or control work, but it has no use when teaching Agility. The idea of the check chain is that it can quickly tighten and slacken round the dogs neck as a method of restraining him, while also conveying the message that he is being corrected. There is no question of correction during jumping training which should have been dealt with while teaching control. I prefer that handlers have a check chain with them so that in between jumping lessons control can be maintained. However, while using any of the Agility equipment they should be wearing a flat leather or nylon collar that does not tighten when tension is applied by the lead. Apart from unnecessary tightening on the dogs neck, a check chain naturally hangs loose when not under tension. This can be dangerous if there are any protuberances on the equipment with which the chain could become entangled.

All successful dog training relies to a certain extent upon the dog gaining confidence that he is doing what is required by his handler. With Agility teaching the dogs confidence takes on an even greater degree of importance for not only does he need to be sure that he is behaving in the required manner, but also confidence on the equipment itself is necessary. Therefore confidence is probably Agility's biggest single training factor. Certainly if the wary handler always bears in mind that any training action that is likely to destroy this trust or instill fear in the dog should be studiously avoided they will not go far wrong. Of course the dog is not going to remain bold when consistently asked to negotiate rocky or unstable equipment, so the handler must ensure that the obstacles are strong and firm.

While there are certain pieces of Agility equipment which for the purpose of training can be grouped together, for me the test that the basics have been properly mastered is the controlled jumping of a hurdle. The way the hurdle, or clear jump, is required to be performed in other dog training sports is a perfect example. Therefore ideally, before progressing on to more difficult equipment, the handler should be able to demonstrate the ability to jump the dog over a 2' 6" high hurdle under perfect control. This will mean facing a hurdle with the dog sitting quietly in the heel position, without a lead attached, until asked to give the dog his jumping command. On the one command he should immediately clear the hurdle, and on a further command remain steady in the stand, sit or down position. The reactions to the commands should be just like pressing the start and stop buttons on a well maintained machine, for in such a way controlled jumping is demonstrated. The reverse would be rushing round a practise Agility course with the dog jumping whilst on the lead, which would do nothing for his control and everything for making him 'jump-happy'. Such a term does not denote the dogs pleasure at jumping, but rather that he will jump anything, be it the obstacle the handler wants him to negotiate or not.

In any book on the subject of dog training, sooner or later the question of the commands to use will always arise. Of course the answer does not vary, for the handler can use any words providing that such words are used consistently. Dog trainers understand that dogs react to sounds rather than words. The words only make sense to humans, but the sounds consistently used will convey a message to the dog. A dog will also very quickly learn to react to signals that are either consciously or unconsciously given. A good example being the display of pleasure given by the dog when his owner pickes up the lead or feeding dish. In such a case the dog has learned what message these items convey and he is therefore only reacting to signals. Situations also induce reactions from dogs. The dog who associates going out in the car with pleasure will probably jump into the car if the door is left open. In other words he has reacted to a given signal, which in this case is the open car door. Such reactions can be used to good effect with the dog being trained for Agility. Many experienced dogs will make the required negotiation of whatever obstacle they are faced with without a command being necessary. All the handler has to do is run towards the obstacle and the dog will react accordingly when he reaches it, be it a tunnel, a dog-walk or hurdle. In such cases the dog is reacting to situations which, providing it is combined with basic control, is to the handlers advantage. On a tricky course where the jumps are close together, without such control disaster can easily strike. There may be two similar obstacles next to each other, only one being the correct one, but the dog sees a situation where either jump is acceptable to him. Therefore the only way to avoid such a disaster is for the handlers control to be good enough to call the dog away from the wrong jump and direct him to the correct one. It should therefore be apparent that it is possible to teach the dog to react to one Agility command which will be effective for all pieces of equipment. Another method is to put the obstacles into three groups using a different command for each group. This is the system that I have used, with the command 'Up' for hurdles, dog-walk, hoop, table, ramp and see-saw. 'Through' for the two tunnels and the weaving poles, and 'Over' for the long jump. This latter obstacle could be placed in the 'Up' command group, but I have sometimes used a separate long jump command for Working Trials as this helps to avoid the possibility of the dog choosing the wrong jump. There are handlers who prefer to use the name of each obstacle as the command so that by constant repetition the dog will identify each obstacle by name. I think this unnecessarily extends the dog's vocabulary which will already be quite extensive. Some handlers use 'In-out, In-out' for the weaving poles while others make a continuous sound until the dog completes them. But the whole point about commands is use what you like. If it works for you who can argue?

What must be remembered is that Agility is not an obedience test so that while many commands and signals can be used, those that are unobeyed will most likely have the effect of penalising the dog anyway, be it by faults or time. It will be a sad day if Agility becomes more like an Obedience test for that would take away a lot of the speed and excitement. If minor handling points were penalised Agility judging would become more obscure. The sport as it is now is understood by spectators, let us hope they are always able to do so.

THE WEAVING POLES

The weaving poles are cunning devices that require little physical exertion from the dog and a considerable amount of practise to achieve reliability. Of all the Agility equipment this one probably causes handlers the most headaches. There are several aids that can be used to get the dog to respond as required. First I will describe methods used during the early days of Agility. They still have their uses but later in this chapter a more advanced training system is explained. It takes longer to teach but the rewards are infinitely greater, which makes it worth while. If the dog has a strong retrieve instinct, then a ball or toy kept just in front of his nose may well persuade him to move through the poles, while the greedy dog will probably react favourably to food or tit-bits. With both such cases the left hand holding a short lead can guide the dog, while the inducement of food or toy is held in the right hand and used much in the same way as the famous carrot on a string in front of a donkey's nose. However in this case the dog's successful weave is rewarded by a play retrieve or being given the food. If the dog under training is not greedy or has no great love for retrieving then the left hand guiding him on a short lead must suffice. In any case the handler can use the left leg to great advantage by nudging the dog between two poles then slightly moving away again and drawing him back between the next two poles by the use of the lead. All this is made much easier if the training poles are low enough to enable the handler to move the lead holding arm backwards and forwards across the top of the poles. I use 4' broom handles cut in half and painted white, with 6" nails partially embedded into the bottom so that the poles are easily erected on a hard grassy surface. With large breeds such as the German Shepherd Dog, slightly longer training poles would be better to avoid the dogs head being higher than the poles.

The handler must always remember to train the dog to only enter the poles in the correct entrance. This is shown in figure 1 and means that the dog should pass the first pole so that it is on the left side of his body before going behind pole 2. The outcome is that the dog will pass pole 3 on his left and pole 4 on his right etc, etc. Any other route is considered as incorrect, bringing penalisation either by time while the handler corrects the mistake, or by faults being added. It makes sense that the training from the beginning should always follow the correct course, for if not the dog can become confused.

A further aid to teaching the weaving poles is for every other pole to be staggered. This is best achieved by setting the poles out in a straight line, 2' apart, and then by moving every other pole out from the original line between 4" to 6", this has the effect of creating a straight channel between both rows of poles which will only require the dog to weave slightly, making teaching so much easier. As he learns, the stagger can gradually be reduced so that eventually the dog is weaving through a straight line of poles. Whatever has been chosen for the command should be used interspersed with 'Good boy' initially every time the dog passes between any two poles that take him away from the handler. It may be impossible if the reader has chosen to use a continuous command, for there will be little time to insert the praise that is so necessary when training dogs. The more commonly used commands are 'Through', 'Weave' or 'Poles' and after much training such as half a dozen attempts twice a day, the dog will learn to do it without lead, toys or food. Training aids are of course still permissible for the handler has the voice, hand signals, leg signals and manner of handling, all of which will add up to assistance for the dog. Of course the handler must remember to avoid 'kneeing' the dog during competition for it will be faulted. It must be accepted that contact between the handlers trousers and the dogs fur could wrongly be construed as 'kneeing', so the training aim should be to allow a gap between handler and dog.

The advanced system of training mentioned earlier in this chapter is for those whose aim is to be able to send the dog into the poles ahead of the handler from any angle to complete a fast accurate weave.

I developed it when teaching Amos on Appro (Moss) in the spring of 1981 having just acquired him as a reject from the Guide Dog for the Blind Association. My previous Agility dog Spot had been taught by the earlier methods which required the handler to be beside the dog. The fact that some handler's leg movements had more in common with a Latin American dance than dog training had little appeal. Therefore it occured to me to devise a method whereby the dog would enter and complete the weaving poles without his handler. With odd refinements the following is the result.

Twelve broom handles approximately 3′ long with 6″ nails partially imbedded in the bottom plus string or stiff wire is all that is required. First set up the twelve poles 21″ apart in a straight line (Fig 2A). Then move every other pole 18″ to the right to form a parallel channel. Be sure to leave the first pole in position so that only even numbered poles are moved to the right (Fig 2B). Either end may be used to start as the result will be the same providing that there is an even number of poles. Fix string or stiff wire between each pole just below the dog's shoulder height, this will create an 18″ wide channel. The dog must now be walked through on a lead so that he has no fear of the

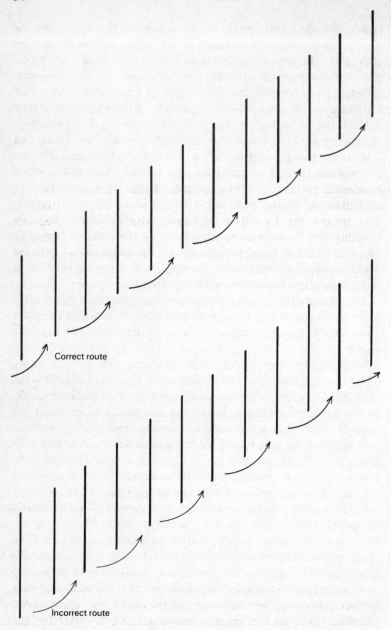

Correct route

Incorrect route

Fig. 1 Weaving poles

channel's restriction. Many dogs will attempt to jump out but the handler must not allow this to happen. It is easily avoided by holding the lead in the left hand almost on the collar fastening. To jump out the dog must rise but the lead held low will not allow him to do so. The same will apply if he tries to go under the string. The whole point is that the dog must not learn that he can get out but rather learn the channel's restriction holds no fear.

In the initial stages the entrance should be from one end only, with a hurdle some five or six yards away from the exit. All handlers look for a short cut. In this case the obvious would be to turn the dog back immediately he exits. This would be a bad habit for continually practised it will always be his exit re-action. Invariably in competition the dog will be required to go on, so from the beginning he should become used to completing all the poles then go on to another obstacle, hence the reason for a hurdle just beyond the exit. Walking the dog through the channel then allowing him to jump the hurdle should be continually practised on as many training sessions as necessary. Until he can be relied upon not to attempt jumping out, no further progress can be made. All dogs vary in the length of time required on training progressions so there is 'no rule of thumb' time guide. When ready to progress call the dog into the 'present' position just inside the channel, so that he is restricted on both sides. Tell the dog to 'Wait' then back away until approximately halfway before calling him into a 'present'. Praise him then repeat the process by backing away to the end before returning round the channel to recommence. If the dog made any attempt to jump out revert to walking him through on the lead, if not, repeat this last procedure four or five times. Where possible speed of movement should be encouraged for speed with control is one of the objectives. Eventually recall the dog along the full length of the channel. The next step is for the dog to start just inside the restrictions with the handler several yards outside the exit but still facing him. After a time he can be started progressively further away from the entrance and being a creature of habit will still go through the channel. Thus confidence has been built to run through the channel to his handler.

Now training is switched to sendaways. If the advice given in an earlier chapter has been followed, the dog will happily go away to his food dish or something much smaller containing a tit-bit. This dish should be placed just outside the channel exit and the dog started inside the restrictions of the entrance. Set him up in a sendaway

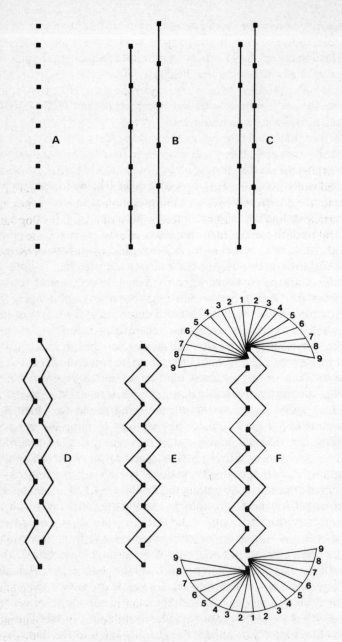

Fig. 2 Advanced weave training

manner prior to giving the command 'Away'. If the previous advice has been adopted the dog will run through to find food which he should be allowed to consume. The hurdle, while still being in place is not used at this stage. Repeat the sequence several times to be sure the dog has the idea then proceed by starting the dog gradually further away from the entrance. Likewise the food dish can be placed progressively further from the exit.

As a training aid the use of food is often overdone so the handler must be aware of such a trap. By now with my own dogs I would have substituted the reward of food with a play retrieve. This must also be carried out with care as timing and accuracy of throw should not distract the dog from weaving. At the psychological moment of exit the article should land just a few feet in front of him. If the dog has a natural retrieve instinct then speed will quickly come and the article can also be thrown over the hurdle. When this stage has been reached and successfully persevered with it is time to commence narrowing the channel (Fig 2C). Each reduction of width should not exceed the thickness of a thumb. In fact it is easy to close down the width too quickly thus encouraging the dog to jump out of the channel and this must be avoided at all costs. Following each width reduction go back to the basic principle of walking him through on the lead so that he has no desire to jump out. If he has, either ensure that you can overcome the problem immediately or revert to the previous width. Eventually the channel becomes too narrow which necessitates making it into a slight zig-zag (Fig 2D). When using string further pieces can be attached to the string between each pole and staked to the ground, this will pull the original strings into a zig-zag shape. If wire has become the training aid a slight bend can now be applied. This is why it was necessary to make the original distance between each pole 21″ so that when maximum bend is applied later the final distance between each pole becomes 18″. Gradually close down the poles to a straight line at the same time increase the angle of the zig-zag so a channel remains (Fig 2E). Remember that each reduction of pole width must be followed by reverting to early methods then building up again. With the throw over the dogs head and subsequent hurdle, speed through and out of the poles will be built up. It is almost time to remove the string or wire but not yet for angles of entry into the poles must now be trained as should entrance from either end. Fig 2F shows the arcs several yards from either end of the poles. These are the positions from where the handler should send the dog on, starting with position number one which is of course a straight on approach followed by numbers two, three and four etc. Before progressing to a greater angle ensure previous ones have been perfected. When certain the dog is ready channel restrictions can be removed from the middle outwards in a gradual progression towards the beginning and end. However, ensure that the dog succeeds at each stage. Always revert to the straight on approach from the number one position as each restriction is removed.

Additionally to teaching the dog to enter ahead of the handler from angles, other starting positions should be practised. In competition the course designs might suit a variety of different handler starting points. To allow for this sometimes start with the dog and run with him as he weaves. This method is often the best for inducing speed of weaving movement.

The recall through the poles is also possible using the string or wire training method. To achieve this it is just a matter of a normal recall by leaving the dog at one end before recalling him through the poles from the other.

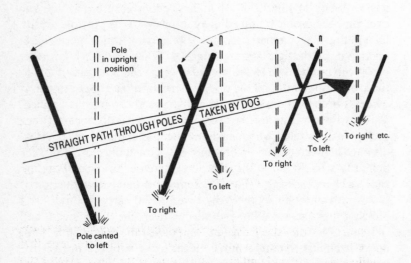

Fig. 3 Another weave method

Another great advantage particularly for those aspiring to double sided handling is being able to do so at the weaving poles. It is quite simple, just run down the left hand side of the poles as often as running down the right.

All manner of starting positions should be practised. In such a way he will never be unsure of what to do when his handler adopts what to other dogs might be a strange position.

Another method of teaching the weave is to start with just two poles encouraging the dog to go through the correct entrance by the use of a play retrieve article. This article is thrown ahead of the dog as he runs between the two poles. When he becomes proficient a third pole can be added If this chapter's has been thoroughly followed by now the dog should have a weave of which you can be proud. A further aid can be to angle every other pole outwards thus creating a natural channel through the middle. Some dogs might learn by this method alone but if the desire is to able to send the dog ahead from any angle to complete a perfect weave it may not be sufficient. Follow word for word the description of training build up I have outlined and if you have the right material, failure is unlikely.

One final word of advice, it could still take up to a year's experience in competition before the dog is almost 100% reliable. I say almost for no one can guarantee 100% success with an animal.

HURDLES

Under this title I class other pieces of equipment such as the brush fence, walls, and any obstacle that will require the dog to clear the jump. I have already stated that for me a controlled jump on this equipment is the basis of all jumping, be it for Working Trials or Agility Tests. I therefore intend to make the assumption that the dog is sufficiently obedient to be left facing the jump while the handler goes to the far side, ensuring that when doing so the lead remains slack. This is a simple matter of having taught the dog to 'sit' and 'wait'. Need it be suggested that if the handler is unable to carry this out satisfactorily, the hurdle should be put away until such time as the basic control has been improved. The English language has many proverbs and sayings and there are two of the most famous that readily spring to mind and aptly apply to dog training. "Don't run before you can walk" and "More haste, less speed". The temptation may be to get on with the jumping, but attention to basic training first will pay great dividends in the future.

The initial height of the top bar on a practise hurdle should be in keeping with the size of dog to be taught so that he only has to hop over. There should also be sufficient other bars to deter the dog from trying to run under rather than jump over. The dog should be sitting facing the hurdle between 12″ and 18″ from it so that as he rises his front legs do not knock off the bars. The handler, having told the dog to 'Wait', can move to the far side, pausing before encouraging the dog to jump. This pause is to avoid anticipation by the dog which will develop if the handler always immediately calls him over. Far better to give a further command 'Wait' while standing still for a second or two, before using the command 'Up' and flicking the lead so that as both hands go towards the groin the dog is encouraged towards the handler. As the dog jumps the handler should back away to allow him room to land, and if all goes well the dog must be praised so that he is aware that his actions have met with approval. If he struggled against the lead movement stubbornly refusing to budge, all is not lost. The next time, rather than the dog being called over the hurdle, the handler can run towards it with the dog at heel on the lead, so that both dog and handler jump over it together. Whilst the 'Up' command can still be used, the run and jump should be made great fun to help the dog lose any fear he may associate with the obstacle. Once this method has been successfully concluded on several occasions the dog should be ready to jump over the low hurdle bar towards his handler. The progression is for the handler to sit the dog in the heel position holding the lead in either hand so as to be able to give a gentle tug on it while giving the 'Up' command. This hand movement will later become a great asset as a signal, allowing the handler to indicate the next jump to be traversed. As the dog lands he should be praised sufficiently to let him know that he has done well, but beware overdoing it which may make him jump back to the handler. Remember that control is now required, so ensure that the dog remains stationary before joining him.

At all times this initial jumping training must be fun, with any compulsion necessary to propel the dog over the hurdle being tempered with praise. Canine bribery such as food can also be used as long as care is taken, for the crafty dog may only work for food, cocking a snoot at his handler if he thinks he is not to be rewarded in this way. As long as the dog jumps it doesn't really matter what method is used to achieve it providing it is firm kindness. Should the handler become frustrated feeling his temper rising, that must be the signal to stop training. Continuance under such circumstances will not educate the dog but only vent the handlers temper on a helpless animal that should never be subjected to human temper.

The aim is to perfect the hurdle at the initial low height commencing with the dog sitting at heel, lead free, then jumping on one command and signal, before remaining steady on the far side. Once this has been regularly achieved the height of the top bar can be raised, 3″ to 6″ at a time, perfecting the dog at each new height until he will happily clear five percent more than the maximum height required in competition. Many dogs are clever enough to judge within fractions of an inch the amount of energy and lift required, and sometimes this can develop into over-confidence, with subsequent misjudgement, meaning that a bar has been knocked off. The extra five percent in practise will not guarantee a dog always jumping clear but it will help to avoid costly knock-downs.

Sometimes even the more experienced dog will become a lazy jumper who does not allow sufficient clearance over the top bar. Often this happens when the dog has become immune to slightly touching lightweight bars that easily roll off. The most likely counter to such behaviour is to use a heavier bar which is not so easily dislodged. When the dog has rapped it once or twice he will have the sense to lift his legs sufficiently to clear it, however care must be taken to ensure that the bar can be dislodged by the dog so that it is not dangerous.

The astute handler should remember to occasionally train the dog to jump the maximum height with just one top bar only. This will leave an inviting space below for the dog to pass under rather than jump, so the handler can re-train him if necessary to ensure he understands that the command really means jump.

The Agility Test rules do not forbid such a hurdle to be used, so it is wise to take out an insurance policy to guard against such a possibility. Don't be like me, forgetting my own advice, so that my own dog in competition ran under a top bar losing the Working Trial qualification as a result.

THE TABLE AND PAUSE

Once the dog has been taught to jump a hurdle on command, teaching him to jump on the table is quite simple for he will have the ability but most likely lack the requisite confidence. The first point to ensure is that the table is of stable construction with a non-slip surface, for the learner dog will quickly distrust anything that wobbles. When the table is constructed in a manner which makes it impossible for the dog to run under it during training, the handler must also train the dog on tables that have no underfilling.

If the handler has already taught the dog to jump onto a table, either for grooming purposes or for convenience at the vets, then whatever has been the method of achieving such obedience should continue to be used for the Agility table. There is no sense in making life difficult by teaching a different method or by using a new command. If this is not so, then stick to the command that has been used to teach hurdle jumping, which for the purpose of this book we will assume is 'Up'. Run towards the table with the lead held in the left hand, then when the table is reached, quickly pat it with the right hand simultaneously giving the command. With luck the dog will jump onto the table or attempt to do so by putting his paws on the top. With both instances the dog must be given immediate praise, either for the success or to encourage him to make the final effort to get his hind legs on as well. Providing he is wearing a plain collar, a little gentle lifting help with the lead will probably be all that is necessary to complete the jump, when more praise should be given. Once he is on the table the handler should concentrate on reassuring the dog that all is well so that he does not jump off until required to do so.

If the previous method does not work the following attempts will require an assistant, preferably a skilled instructor. While the dog is held by the assistant the handler can go to the far side of the table, ensuring that the dog can still be seen. As the assistant lets go, the command 'Up' can be given while patting the table. Should the dog attempt to run round or under, the next move is for the handler to kneel on the far side of the table going through the same procedure of commanding the dog who should start on the opposite side. If failure still persists, the handler can stand on the table before giving the command and some gentle lead assistance, which will probably have the desired effect. The final answer with the awkward dog is for the assistant to lift him on to the table which the handler is kneeling upon. One of these methods is sure to work if correctly carried out. Just remember that the dog will in all probability be only too pleased to comply once he knows what is required and has the confidence to try.

Do not attempt to make the dog stand, sit or go down on the table, but rather allow him to do what he wishes, which must not include jumping off again until told to do so.

Once the dog has jumped on the table several times, then the training progression is for the handler to approach it with the dog under control, giving the command and patting signal when reached. As progress is made with the dog happily jumping on the table without lead assistance, the pat on the table should become an indication signal without actual contact being made with the equipment.

If the basic control has been correctly instilled into the dog, the final part can be quite simple. It will be a matter of the command 'Up' followed by 'Down' for this is the position the dog will be required to adopt in most competitions.

The handlers control should be such that the dog can be sent ahead towards the table while giving the two commands from behind him. The handler continues to run on past the table until reaching the next obstacle at which the dog will recommence. Such handling not only shows control but can save vital seconds.

The pause box is not as often used as the table. It is usually a 4' square laid on the ground in which the dog is required to go down. The immediate down again comes into its own for if the basic control has been correctly taught no further teaching is required. The dog that will not remain in the down position for five seconds should resume basic down training. Seconds lost on the table or pause box cannot be afforded.

THE 'A' RAMP

Originally referred to as a scale jump but now called the 'A' ramp or 'A' frame this official name distinguishes it from the vertical scale used in other competitions. The scale jump has come under much discussion in the past. Some people maintain that continually jumping off the top of a scale jump onto hard ground can damage a dog's shoulders. I have an open mind on the subject for I am not a veterinary surgeon and no one in Great Britain has produced documentary evidence to either prove or disprove the theory. Whilst it is not the purpose of this book to judge other sports equipment, I mention it only to bring home the fact that the Agility ramp does not have a dangerous landing factor. Even if the dog has been incorrectly taught and jumps off four feet from the bottom, the angle of the jump means that he is landing from a lesser height which has little difference to a hurdle landing. An added safety factor is that both sides of the ramp have coloured areas covering the last 3'6". They are referred to as contact points therefore judges expect at least a part of one paw to make contact, if not, the dog is given five faults. It has the effect of making handlers teach their dogs to traverse the whole of each side of the 'A' ramp. This is an accepted practice, thus ensuring that the 'A' ramp will neither cause canine shoulder damage nor be viewed with the same suspicion as the vertical scale. Having explained the importance of the contact points, the reader will fully understand why I shall stress, that from the beginning, 'A' ramp training must include running the dog down all the way to the ground.

There are many ways to teach the 'A' ramp, but as not every reader will have a ramp of their own or even the facilities to erect one that is full sized, I shall deal first with a cheap and easy way to get started. In most towns someone sells second-hand interior hard-board or plywood doors. They are usually damaged and are therefore suitably cheap for our purpose. Two butt hinges will join the doors together and four or five wooden slats can be nailed across the sides of the exterior. Even if the doors are constructed of hardboard there is usually a narrow frame on the two long sides to which the slats can be nailed. Most doors are approximately 6'6" long, so that when the two joined doors are laid out on the ground the length is about 13′. The dog, on a lead, can be walked backwards and forwards over the doors which will accustom him to traversing them. They can then be slightly raised and secured by hammering two stout pegs into the ground at the base on both sides. These pegs will ensure that the doors do not slip down again, with only one side having to be reset each time the height and angle is altered. In such a way a cheap, light and easy training ramp is made, but the handler must take care to ensure that it is stable enough for the dog under training. If not the dog may distrust it, so that rather than building confidence it is being diminished.

Some of the large 'A' ramps used that conform to Agility regulations can also be raised and lowered for teaching purposes, but as most training classes have only one model, this can be inconvenient. It is only in rare cases that it is absolutely necessary to start the dog scaling with the angle and height severely reduced, as most dogs will take to scaling the full height quite easily. The greatest problem to be found when teaching on this equipment erected to competition standards is the height of the handler. The apex of the ramp is 6′3″ from the ground, which often leaves the shorter person, particularly ladies, with a problem. However, a short lady with a willing dog will not experience too much trouble, but if the method next described does become difficult because of a lack of height, there are other ways that may be successful.

The dog should be wearing a plain collar as opposed to a check chain, and secured on a short lead he can be run towards the ramp. An important factor is that as the handler reaches the ramp he should be as close as possible to the side of it so that there is no room for the dog to run by. The lead should be held in the left hand, with the right hand remaining free to be used as a signal, patting the ramp ahead of the dog. This action will compliment the command 'Up', which if correctly learned during hurdle training, will quickly convey to the dog what is required. However the danger point is two thirds of the way up where many dogs will consider it easier to jump off rather than to continue to struggle upwards. As long as the handler is aware that this is likely to happen and is close enough to the ramp to make it impossible, further encouragement and gentle persuasion will get the dog to the top. Once the dog has reached the apex the handler must immediately concentrate on getting him to run all the way down the far side rather than allowing premature jumping off several feet before the bottom is reached. It has already been explained that a dog, being a creature of habit, will be more likely to follow the same route as previously taken. When asked to try again it becomes obvious that the first attempt should have ensured that the dog ran all the way to the bottom of the ramp making it easier to insist that he does so in future. During the first attempts the handler must remember to use praise so that the dog is able to understand he is reacting in the required manner.

Should the dog have put up a struggle in excess of the handlers strength, or if the handlers lack of height has been a problem, then providing the ramp is of sturdy construction it can be climbed by the handler. When this method is employed it is preferable for an assistant, or better still an experienced instructor, to handle the dog while the owner climbs the far side of the ramp until at least his head and shoulders are in view of the dog. At this point the owner should call the dog in an excited manner using his name and the recall command. Simultaneously the assistant should run him towards the ramp so that he has the impetus to climb. With this system the assistant acts as the handler, running close to the jump and keeping firm pressure on the lead before passing it to the owner to take over. In all but the most stubborn cases this method will bring positive results, but if not it is still possible for the owner to be more in view sitting to one side astride the top of the ramp. Of course if all else fails it will be a question of lowering the ramp height and angle until it is such that the dog will accept it without a great struggle.

As with all jumping the handler must remember that it is unlikely the dog is just being awkward or stubborn, but rather that he lacks the confidence to try. It is the handlers job to ensure that this confidence is instilled and that other than reasonable physical persuasion to go up and over, nothing is done which may frighten him. By virtue of its size the 'A' ramp looks difficult but it is one of the easier pieces of equipment that the dog will need to master.

TUNNELS

The collapsible tunnel and the pipe tunnel are two obstacles that are not difficult for the dog to negotiate. In fact the collapsible type is usually such great fun for the dog that once mastered he may want to tunnel other than when required to do so. In view of this and the fact that it is more easily shortened than the pipe tunnel, the dog is best first taught on the collapsible version. When this has been accomplished the other tunnel will hold no fear for the dog, who will run through it without a second thought.

Tunnel training is initially a two person operation with the assistant or skilled instructor holding the dog at the entrance. The handler
should go to the far end gathering four or five feet of the material
into the hands so that the tunnel is shortened. It should then be held
in such a fashion that it is an open tube with the handlers head
framed in the exit so that his dog can see him. If the handler has first
told the dog to go down in the tunnel entrance it will help him see the
person he trusts. By using whatever command or encouragement is
most effective, it is just a case of the handler calling the dog through
while the assistant must ensure that the dog does not attempt to run
round the tunnel when called. Holding the lead until sure that the
dog is going to run through will help to stop this possibility, plus
giving the added advantage of being able to keep his head low
enough to see his handler. Once the dog is tunnelling, the assistant,
as he drops the lead, should stand in the tunnel entrance ensuring
that the dog cannot return the way he entered. As the dog emerges at
the far end he should be given lavish praise before being returned to
the assistant for a repeat performance. After several such successful

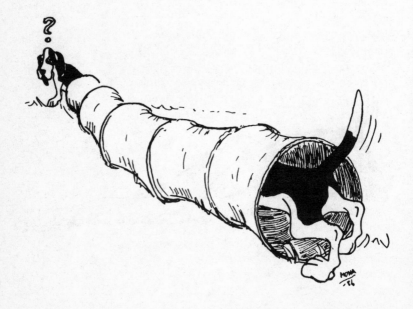

attempts the handler can drop the cloth on the dogs back as he starts moving so that he becomes accustomed to pushing his way through the material. Once this stage has been reached the next step is for the owner to be with the dog as he enters the tunnel. As the dog starts to move through the owner should be encouraging him from a position that ensures he hears the voice he trusts from ahead rather than behind him. This system will quickly teach the dog to have no fear of the collapsible tunnel whilst also ensuring that he will run through any confined area such as the pipe tunnel.

One word of warning. Most of the collapsible tunnels I have come across require straightening each time a dog has run through. If this is not done there is a risk that the slight disturbance of the cloth will make it twist when the next dog attempts it, with the result that he will become entangled. It is therefore the handlers responsibility to always ensure the cloth is straight before asking the dog to tunnel. Remember that the handler is trying to instil confidence into the dog which becomes difficult each time he becomes entangled.

Where the dog likes to retrieve, then an article thrown ahead of him as he exits can induce more speed. the anticipation of the chase will therefore quicken his movement through the tunnel. Agility is about control combined with speed, so any training method that saves seconds or fractions of them should be tried.

If the dog has only been trained on tunnels made of material that readily admits light he may refuse when faced with a tunnel that is totally dark. It will only affect a proportion of dogs but to ask any dog to go into a dark unknown opening without prior education is asking for trouble. It must also be remembered that some tunnels are constructed of very stiff heavyweight material so such a possibility should also be trained for.

THE HOOP

The hoop is usually a tyre suspended from a substantial frame which the dog is expected to jump through. Whilst it is little more than a hurdle jumped with a greater degree of accuracy, most dogs first reaction is one of refusal unless it is lowered until it touches the ground. In such a way the dog can have his initial training in the same manner as used to teach the hurdle. The dog should be left sitting on one side of the hoop while the handler goes to the far side having passed the lead through in the first place. Using the command 'Up' while flicking the lead the dog can be encouraged to walk through, thus learning that this circular object is not to be feared. After several such successful walks through, the tyre can gradually be raised until it becomes necessary to use something to block the inviting space below the underside. If the dog has already been taught to hurdle a solitary top bar it is less likely that he will attempt to run under the raised hoop, but it will still remain a possibility.

Before the full height is achieved the handler should be sending the dog through on command starting with the dog at heel instead of calling him through as a recall. The initial recall method was only to build up confidence that he was not jumping to somewhere strange.

The handler should always ensure that the hoop is suitably fixed so that it cannot swing or twist, for the dog must learn to trust it or he will not jump with confidence.

There is very little to hoop jumping once the hurdle has been mastered, but the handler must remember that the dog will have to gauge maximum and minimum jumping heights to pass through easily. To do so he will need to learn the exact take-off point required, and for reasons of safety, once mastered it is better to maintain the maximum height rather than lower it.

THE DOG WALK & CROSS OVER

The dog walk is constructed so that it is 9″ to 10″ wide. Whilst a minority of dogs will quite boldly attempt this piece of equipment when first asked to do so, there is also the other extreme of the dog that must first be taught to walk along a narrow board that is only several inches above the ground. Luckily such dogs are few and far between for surprisingly it is easier to teach the dog to walk a plank at 4' 6" high than it is when he is much nearer to the ground. At very low heights his temptation to jump off is greater, for no doubt he sees little point struggling along a narrow board when he could easily walk along the ground. This is much the same principle as the dog faced for the first time with a single bar hurdle, for if he has any sense he will run under rather than jump over. For this reason it makes sense to see what initial reactions the dog will have when asked to ascend the walk.

To proceed the dog should be wearing a plain leather collar and handled on a short lead. An assistant, whose main object will be to ensure that the dog does not jump off, should be on the opposite side of the dog. Approaching the ramp of the dog walk in a straight line, the trio of handler, dog and assistant should continue without pausing, for with the handler and assistant keeping very close to the plank the dog is left with the options of refusing to budge or walking up the ramp. The command 'Up' can be used as he reaches the bottom of the ramp, but at this stage more emphasis should be placed upon assuring him that all is well by speaking in a soothing manner. The free hand can stroke him while the assistant also encourages by patting and indicating the plank in front. Some dogs will accept this method of learning without any fuss, but as already stated such dogs are in a minority. It is much more likely that the dog will refuse to move even though gentle lead pressure is applied. Why should the sensible dog want to move for it will appear to him that he must struggle up a plank to go nowhere. At this point he must be given an incentive to move, which can be done by taking him to the last two or three feet of the walk before the point where the downward ramp is attached. The handler should lift the dog onto the walk so that he is in the position of just looking over the edge at the ramp that he must descend to reach the ground. Remember that all efforts are being concentrated upon giving him confidence, so although the assistant may be the stronger, the handler should be the one to lift the dog rather than a strange person. Of course the assistant should still be close up on the other side of the walk taking care to keep his face away from the dogs head, for although I have not yet seen it happen, a nervous dog excessively worried on the walk could snap at an unfamiliar person.

Both handler and assistant should keep the dog still for a while, fondling him while talking in a reassuring and soothing manner. The aim must be to calm any ideas of panic so that he can see there is nothing to worry about. Once it is felt that the dog is reacting favourably, inch by inch he can be encouraged to descend, with the handler still holding him on a short lead directly above his head. Both people must continue to act as barriers to inhibit attempts at jumping off, with the handler ensuring that the dog walks to the bottom rather than missing out the last three or four feet by jumping ahead to the ground. If the descent was successful it can be repeated by starting at the same downward point or by moving two or three feet further back before lifting him on again. This will give the dog a short piece of level board to walk before descending, and gradually he can be lifted on at points further back until the ascent ramp is reached. It is better at this stage not to try to start half way up the ramp but rather revert to approaching the start of the ramp in a trio as originally attempted.

A very essential part of dog walk training is for the lead to be held above the dogs neck. He has a far better sense of balance than us which means the handler is only upsetting that balance if even slight sideways lead pressure is applied. In fact the quicker the lead can be dispensed with the better, for in unskilled hands it becomes a positive hinderance.

A common mistake made is for the handler to approach the dog walk at an angle, making the initial ascent more difficult than necessary. It makes sense for the dog walk to be approached square on, for doing so can only help the dog to understand that he is expected to climb.

A vital part of the training on this piece of equipment must be ensuring that at all times the dog descends to the bottom rather than leaping off. The last 3' of both ends of this obstacle will be painted a different colour, usually yellow. This indicates the contact points which means the dog must make contact with it by at least part of one paw, otherwise he will be faulted. If the dog under training will respond instantly to the immediate down command it may be possible to drop him on the downward slope, thus giving the handler time to be in a position to stop him jumping off early. Also the handler can stand facing the end of the ramp, close enough to be able to call the dog into the 'present' position without him being able to jump off. Certainly the handler should take any action to ensure that the dog always walks to the very bottom during training, for when on the equipment at speed as will happen when competing, the dog will probably miss out two feet more than he has been allowed to in training.

The cross over whilst not often used is part of approved equipment, It is no more than an elaborate dog walk that has four planks touching the ground attached to a high table in the middle. The handler whose dog has mastered basic obedience and is confident on the dog walk will not have any trouble with this piece of equipment.

THE SEE-SAW

To the dog the see-saw will look no different than the ramp of the dog walk. Whereas the dog walk should be a completely stable piece of equipment, the see-saw is not. A dog has a natural fear of anything unstable, so if his fear for the unsteady is combined with the apprehension of walking up a narrow plank, the degree of difficulty has been doubled. Therefore the dog walk should always be taught first, for in such a way the apprehension for a narrow plank will already have been overcome, leaving just the tipping motion to be mastered.

Whilst for the awkward dog an assistant can be gainfully employed to stop him from jumping off the opposite side, if the dog walk has been completely mastered so that there is no fear of apprehension on a narrow plank, help may be unnecessary. Wearing a plain collar with a short held lead attached to the top, the equipment should be approached square on. As with the dog walk, rather than stopping as the see-saw is reached, by gentle lead pressure it is preferable to ensure that there is a continuing forward movement by the dog who must now start to climb. As he does so the handler should give the command 'Up' followed by reassuring praise until he reaches the point where the distribution of his weight starts the tipping motion. The handler's right hand having been used to encourage the dog prior to the tip, must be under the plank at approximately the point where dog's front feet will tip the scales. By doing so, the handler controls the tip in such a way that it will be executed in a very slow, even manner, while the dog having been told to 'Wait' is held standing still at the tipping point. He will also need much reassurance while the plank is moving, and the handler must be aware that his most likely reaction will be to get off if he can. The slow, even lowering of the plank plus the vocal reassurance while being held in position, will ensure that this does not happen.

Until the tip is complete, there should not be any question of allowing the dog to walk down. In fact it is preferable to continue to hold the dog steady for a second or two so that he realises the board is no longer moving, thus diminishing any apprehension he may have. It must be understood by the handler that after several attempts the dog will be able to judge to the inch the point at which he has previously been stopped. If the handler has erroneously and consistently stopped him prior to the tipping point then this is what the dog has been taught and he will continue to stop prematurely. Therefore until the handler feels the far under side of the plank tip on to his right hand the dog must not be stopped, the aim being to teach him to climb the see-saw, momentarily stop while it tips, then run down the plank to the bottom. If the dog is not taught to stop and subsequently attempts the see-saw at speed, the tip will be so fast that he is left paddling in mid-air as the plank crashes down.

Having ensured that the plank drops smoothly to the ground, walking the dog all the way to the bottom has just as much significance with the see-saw as it did with the dog walk. The 3′ contact point is also found on both sides of this piece of Agility equipment, and the dog will be expected to have at least part of one paw on it.

THE LONG JUMP

This piece of equipment is almost the same as the long jump to be found at other competitions. I say almost, for whilst the construction is the same, the fact that five or six feet length is likely to be the maximum during Agility competitions does tend to make it somewhat easier than the nine feet which the larger dogs are required to clear at Trials. Nevertheless in my opinion it ranks as one of the more difficult Agility jumps for the dog has many ways of tackling it incorrectly. For example he can refuse, run by, step between boards, knock them down, jump in and out at an angle.

Some dogs will take to the long jump without any compulsion being necessary. If they have already mastered the hurdle then placing one unit of the long jump in front of them and, inviting them to jump across it with the hurdle command, might be all that is necessary. From then on a logical progression is to gradually add more units and practise until satisfied the dog understands how to clear this obstacle.

It stands to reason that for dogs that do not respond to the above method a careful build up is necessary, and to do so the handler should commence with just two or three boards close together so that the dog will be asked to jump approximately 3'. Using the command 'Over' or continuing to use the 'Up' command, the handler should run towards the long jump with the dog secured on just sufficient lead to give him mobility at the same time as allowing control. As the jump is reached the command can be repeated as the handler runs down the right hand side, gently lifting the dog to propel him over. Once the dog is airborne the lead can be slightly slackened so that he is not too restricted, then as he lands lavish praise upon him, for the compulsion to propel him over may have falsely indicated that he has done wrong. If successful, repeat this system several times before attempting to lengthen the jump by opening the boards wider or inserting additional ones. Remember that the dog must be allowed to gain his confidence, so make haste slowly, never allowing him to run through the boards. If he does so, next time the lead should be slightly shortened with more lift being used, thus ensuring that it becomes impossible for his feet to touch the ground until he is on the far side. The training can continue on the lead until 5' or 6' have been mastered, but the real test will be for the dog to happily jump lead-free. If he has jumped 6' with the aid of the lead, the wise handler will reduce the length considerably for the first lead-free long jumping attempt. It is also a good initial ruse to surrepticiously unclip the lead a split second prior to jumping, but continue to handle the lead in a manner that makes the dog think he is still attached and has no option but to jump.

Do not expect the dog to learn to long jump lead-free in one session as it is unlikely to be the case. Six or seven attempts per session are quite sufficient and they should always be rewarded with praise, food or play retrieves, for long jump training is essentially very compulsive.

The water jump is no more than a different version of a long jump which may well have a low bar across the front or middle. Certainly such a bar is an advantage for the initial teaching but really once the long jump has been mastered there is little for the handler to fear with water jumps.

OTHER OBSTACLES

Other obstacles may be encountered such as the wishing well or lychgate but once the dog has mastered the hurdles and the hoop this type of obstacle will not be a problem.

4

Course Handling

Having taught the dog good control and how to negotiate the obstacles there is still much to be learned before man and dog become a fluent partnership. Certain basic rules should be observed which avoid later problems. For example there is little point in running the dog around a complete practice course attached to a lead because otherwise he may run off. In this case he will continue to run off or disobey once the lead is dispensed with. There might be an argument for the perfectly controlled dog being run on a lead, but if possible it is to be avoided. A lead can be very dangerous, easily becoming snagged on equipment, especially when in unskilled hands.

Another trap to fall into is the eagerness to practice complete courses. With the vast majority of dogs it is totally unnecessary and in some cases detrimental to the dogs final speed. Never risk allowing the dog to become bored by too much repetition but rather do everything to create enthusiasm. My answer is to start by linking two or three obstacles together maybe gradually adding others over several training sessions. If required the final part of such training can be full practice courses. However this is something I rarely ever do even with an experienced dog. It is far better just to practice the obstacles that have not been perfected, or the combination of obstacles that were a problem at the last official event.

Keep courses and obstacles simple for the learner dog. Make sure equipment he walks over is stable, if not the slightly worried dog can be given greater apprehension. Ensure at least five paces between obstacles particularly hurdles so it is not difficult to land and take off again. The tyre should be kept at the same height which at this stage should be maximum. Dogs learn how to project themselves through the narrow opening at a given height. To alter that height makes it more difficult. The unenlightened have previously lowered the height of the tyre for Junior competition in the mistaken belief that it is easier. They achieved just the opposite making it more difficult so that the dog did not know his take off point. Similar problems face the inexperienced dog when weaving. Poles set apart at distances greater or less than that which he is used to will not help him learn to avoid mistakes. Poles set at irregular intervals also cause problems. Such training ploys whilst being acceptable for the experienced dog are more likely to make learners a little wary resulting in being slower at this obstacle. Speed through the poles must be encouraged as seconds or parts of seconds saved can make all the difference.

Always ensure that the collapsible tunnel is straight. A learner dog becoming tangled can quickly form an association of unpleasantness with this obstacle if trapped. Remember it is a good idea for the handler to check before starting.

The handler must understand the dogs temperament for only the toughest dogs can be chastised whilst on or near the equipment. Very gentle use of the word 'No' may be acceptable for the dog that suffers from any stress on Agility equipment, conversely a very harsh growled 'No' might be better for the tough dog. Between these two extremes are many degrees of verbal chastisement. The art of good training is to know just what is right for any particular dog. However, if possible, never let the dog do anything wrong then it becomes unnecessary to chastise. That of course is the perfect dog training world in which none of us live. Nevertheless to try and achieve it must be an aim.

Never allow the dog to take any obstacle of his choice without command or signal having been given. One may think it fun at first but beware of teaching a bad habit. At any time the dog attempts to do so, stop him quickly by whatever method is right for him. If this rule is not followed and the dog is keen expect him to be frequently eliminated in the ring for 'wrong course'. Likewise the very shy or worried dog that runs out of the ring to a family member or friend can develop such a habit. This must be firmly but very gently stopped.

Extreme angles from one obstacle to another for the learner dog are to be avoided. There will be plenty of time later for practising more acute angles. Preferably at the early stage keep everything

The author and Amos on Appro (Moss).

Hurdle lessons.

Learning the Table.

The perfect weave – fast, without handler assistance.

Weaving Pole progression.

Learning the Tyre.

Initial 'A' Ramp training – upside.

'A' Ramp training – downside.

Don Horsfall helps with the Dog Walk.

Peter and Don control the See-Saw tip.

'A' Ramp contact with food.

Dog Walk contact (note handler position).

John Gilbert and Peter discuss course building.

Burridge Dog Training Club Team qualify for Crufts 1989.

Gwyn Roberts with Tweed.

Barry Harvey and Charles Harvest Sun.

Neville Watson and Heronfleet Balou take off.

Julie Cooper and W.T.Ch. Julie's Judd.

Bill Chuter and Odeon Nesta Square.

A Judging Seminar in Switzerland.

On to the Table (Switzerland).

First attempt at the See-Saw (Switzerland).

Big dogs as well (Switzerland).

Encouraging the dog to descend (Switzerland).

Handler learns the method (Switzerland).

Agility in Germany.

Agility in Holland.

Judging in Denmark.

Agility in Belgium.

Mini action in Belgium.

A flying French mini.

fluent and therefore fast.

COMMANDS AND SIGNALS

Use of commands and signals in practice or competition is critical. The handler has to decide how to indicate successive obstacles on the course so the dog understands. As already mentioned in an earlier chapter there are those who prefer to name each obstacle as a command. I feel this to be an unnecessary enlargement of the dogs vocabulary. But also how does the dog know which of the three inviting hurdles is the next one when commanded 'Hurdle'? For me 'Up', 'Through' and maybe 'Over' are sufficient combined with hand signals to indicate what is next required. Add to this other necessary commands such as 'Wait' or 'Stay', 'Heel', 'Come', 'No', 'Down', 'Away', or 'Go on' perhaps even 'Walk on'. It is all a lot for the dog to assimilate so I keep it simple.

'Wait' or 'Stay' will be required when starting and maybe at the pause. Some also use it on the contact pieces of equipment to momentarily hold the dog in a given position. 'Heel' and 'Come' are quite obvious but what is less obvious is the timing of their use if the dog is likely to take the wrong course. If he is a quick dog a command given as he moves towards the wrong obstacle is far too late. The message needs time to be formulated on the handlers lips, travel to the dogs ears, be sent to his brain for onward transmission to his legs. While this is going on he may have taken several strides in the wrong direction. In such cases do not blame the dog but the handler for being too late with commands. For example, having traversed a hurdle with a trap directly ahead of him the command should have been given when the dog was irrecoverably committed to that previous hurdle. That in effect is a split second before he takes off which gives time for the message to reach his feet as he lands. Just as in tracking dogs the handler must learn to read their own dog. This will mean understanding what he is doing on the course at all times and learning to know what he will do under given circumstances. If he becomes 'tunnel happy', many dogs do, the tunnel, whilst not a trap for others, is a trap for this particular dog. The time to deliver the command that will stop him taking that wrong tunnel is as soon as possible before he sees it.

The command 'No' is self explanatory. 'Down' however might be used to drop the dog at a difficult part of the course that may involve elimination if not stopped. Possibly this command delivered whilst the dog is at full speed will check him but he may not actually drop. This will inevitably allow the handler to regain control of the situation. But beware, using this tactic often without requiring the dog to adopt a prone position can mean he needs more than one command on the table. Forewarned is forearmed! On this subject it is interesting to note that the majority of shepherds use the command 'Lie Down' to their dog whilst working moving sheep. Rarely do they respond instantly requiring several commands to drop. However the shepherd often uses the command just to check the dog which is exactly what we have been discussing.

'Away' or 'Go on' are really sendaway commands which should be used in such a context. Obviously if at any time the handler wants the dog to work on particularly towards the finish is when such a command comes into its own.

Signals allied to commands also have their uses. It makes sense to give directional signals that back up commands when manoeuvring the dog around a course. If handling double sided the dog must be used to signals from both arms. Also it is advisable to give signals with the arm nearest the dog. Remember, if he is on the left with the right arm being used for a signal some of that signal may be masked by the handlers body.

The use of directional control signals as explained earlier certainly come into their own when working the dog around a course.

There is a negative side to signals which are those conveyed to the dog, albeit unwittingly. Some dogs are extremely conscious of body movements particularly collies. Great care must be taken with such dogs. Handlers need to constantly be aware of their hand, chest and shoulder movements for dogs can read all sorts of unwanted messages from such actions. The handler who leaves his dog at the start, moves up the course and while turning to face the dog involuntarily moving an arm can unknowingly signal the dog to start. If this happens often the act of turning to face him will always be a sufficient signal that he will react to.

There are very quick dogs who, when being steadied on the way to down side contacts, respond to body signals. Such dogs may react to the handlers chest movement which is merely inhaling air resulting in the dog's premature departure. This is of course an extreme example but explains just how much care should be taken. The penalty in any event is five faults. All such points must be taken into consideration for signals can be of great assistance or a disaster.

THE START AND PAUSE

To be able to leave the dog at the start line whilst taking up a position past the first or second obstacle to save breath and legs has to be an advantage. Not all courses allow such handling to be possible while others will mean the handler can position himself a greater number of obstacles ahead. Usually something between the two extremes is to be found. We have discussed in Chapter 2 the use of good control. Here is a classic example of its use, a firm command 'Wait' backed up by a hand signal before moving confidently away. If as previously suggested recalling the dog over hurdles has been part of his training, it is now quite simple to call him to you using the requisite command each time he approaches an obstacle. The next decision is when to move away for the handler needs time to obtain speed to have any chance of matching that of the dogs. Usually it should be as the dog commits himself to the hurdle. When moving away allowance should be made for the side on which the dog is to be when they come together. Moving off before the dog becomes a temptation for the handler to turn his back upon him. This is not so bad if the head is twisted back to keep him in vision.

Agility is not far removed from any of the ball games. The basic rule they all have is 'never take your eyes of the ball'. As soon as that happens you are in trouble. In our case the dog becomes the ball who should never disappear from our vision for even a split second.

Those who take part in agility will no doubt recall constant incidences of eliminations, all because the handler lost sight of the dog or deliberately gambled. Often the inexperienced will assume the dog will take the next jump and therefore continue on the course oblivious to the fact that he has run round the obstacle following his handler.

There is an art in positioning the dog at a start. If the first or second obstacle is at an angle to the start line it may be advantageous to position the dog to one side or the other. When manual timing is used starting the dog on the line can be an advantage if the timer appears a little slow in his reactions. If the timer does not appear slow position the dog at least one yard behind the line so that he has gained momentum when he crosses it. This definitely applies to electronic timing which the handler must remember to walk round when leaving the dog at the start. Bear in mind that most judges will not allow a false start in a singles competition for, after coming under timers orders, once the dog crosses the line timing commences.

Another point to be beware of is when there is a spread fence as number one obstacle. If this is as close as five paces from the start then considerable extra starting distance will be beneficial to the dog. This can be gained by leaving him further back.

The pause is really a question of good basic obedience being put together in Agility. If it is a table or box pause an immediate 'Down' followed by 'Wait' or the usual command will allow the handler five seconds to gain a little more ground or move into a good position further up the course. Precious seconds or even one hundredth of a second can be saved in this manner. They all count.

HANDLING ON BOTH SIDES

Until the first edition of this book was published in 1981 the vast majority of competitors handled their dogs on their left hand side. This is the conventional side from which to work a dog. Throughout the world, and certainly in Great Britain, Obedience or Control is taught with the dog on the left. During the early eighties I was handling my Border Collie Spot on both sides switching at will to the most advantageous side as we progressed around a course. Some people were astounded and there were even a few who felt it unfair. Still the most common method of handling is the dog well trained to the heel position with dog and handler setting off together and at all times retaining the relative heel position. At obstacles, the gap between handler and dog becomes greater to allow the dog to traverse the obstacles without the handler. Once the obstacle has been completed, then the reasonably close heel position is resumed. This is without doubt the least complicated method of handling an agility dog. Its advantages are that the handler always knows where the dog will be, and within reason is less likely to have the dog totally out of vision. Many prizes are won by competitors in this manner. The disadvantages are that the competitor must run all the way round a course. Often parts of the course will bend in such a manner that the handler is actually running a greater distance than the dog. Needless to say one needs to be pretty fit if such a method is to be used.

There is certainly nothing wrong with handling the dog all the way in the heel position, in fact some of the most prolific agility winners handle in this way. Its greatest advantage is in its simplicity. There is less chance to get in a muddle, and certainly less planning of how the course should be attacked. One might think this is the method I prefer, but I have never seen any point in running as far as, or greater distances than, the dog. As one becomes a little older and perhaps wiser as a dog handler, the less running necessary the better. Much running distance can be saved by working the dog on the left or right, whichever is applicable at that point of the course.

At some stage or another, it will usually be part of the plan to change handling sides and here considerable skill is required. The handler must decide whether to change sides in front or behind the dog. If to do so means stopping the dog's impetus, then changing handling sides becomes counter-productive. In this manner one may save ground, but the clock will continue to tick.

At this stage I would not blame you if the reaction was to say "this all sounds too difficult for me. I will use the heel position method." The only question I would pose is that if you start by handling only with the dog in the heel position, you are less likely to be able to change later should you wish to. On the other hand, if able to handle in a more flamboyant manner, it is quite simple to also decide to handle with the dog on the left all the way round when applicable.

Working the dog on the left should not give the handler undue problems providing that basic control was correctly taught. If so, the handler should already be quite comfortable with the dog on the left side. Maybe too comfortable, so that when asked to work him from the other side everything feels difficult. It is quite easily overcome providing the handler works at it.

Start by placing the dog in the heel position in front of a hurdle that he has just cleared several times. Tell the dog to sit wait, then go to his other side so that the dog is now on the right. Giving the appropriate signal and command send the dog over. If he should attempt to run into the heel position, it may be necessary temporarily to revert to doing this on the lead. Once he has the idea, repeat the sequence on several occasions. If he is able to progress, put up a second hurdle on line to the first one. Proceed in the same manner and then, when satisfied that all is well, string both jumps together running past the first one while the dog jumps it on your right hand side.

It is just a matter of building up from there, as all obstacles can eventually be worked in such a manner. It is not difficult, only

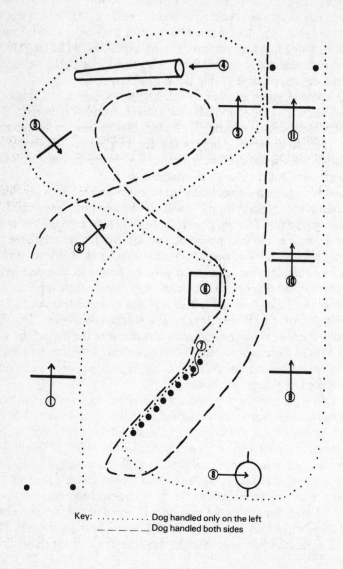

Key: . . . . Dog handled only on the left
———— Dog handled both sides

Fig. 4 Olympia 1980 final

requiring patient logical build up.

Remember that dogs learn to recognise signals, even those the handler is unaware of. The use of the arm and hand must be studied carefully. For example, if up until now the dog has only worked left handed, maybe the handler has consistently used the same arm and/or hand to convey a message. When working the dog on the other side, it then becomes important that the opposite arm and hand is used to produce a balanced effect.

All this needs to be included in the initial attempts to work the dog on both sides. If not, a somewhat confused dog that is unsure of the position required will be the result.

For those not averse to the use of food, tit bits can help to distract him from being aware he is in a strange position in relation to the handler.

It is a matter of common sense of building up the dog's and one's own confidence. Practise until on the same course it is possible to handle all the way round with the dog on a given side. When this feels comfortable, then the time has come to change sides during a run.

Work out an obvious plan to change sides behind the dog on one part of the course. It is always far easier to do so behind the dog so that he is not distracted from what he is doing. Again the advantage of the dog being able to work forward comes into play, for if he will not do so then the handler cannot change sides behind him.

It should now be possible to change sides several times during a course and under virtually any circumstances. If so, you have become a double-sided handler. You will have more breath in reserve at the end of the course, more options about how to handle and greater possibilities of masking the dog's view of the course trap.

One problem will now always remain. There are so many options open to you as a dual-sided handler that your task is going to be greater than the left handers. They know the dog will always be on the left, and therefore when walking the course decisions are that much easier. You will have to make many decisions mainly about when and where to change sides.

If having made the plan, something goes wrong during the round, then improvisation will be that much more involved. Do not however be disturbed. Your reward is probably improved course times which must be in your interest.

After all what is it all about? No course faults and the fastest time. Maybe it will help you to become a winner. If it does let me be the first to congratulate you.

WORKING ON

Having taught all the obstacles and ensured that the dog will work confidently on either side progress can be continued. Putting it all together so that it looks and feels fluent is not as easy as it appears. To watch a fast, smooth, quietly handled round can be likened to a work of art. Man and dog in perfect harmony. It looks so simple but much work will have been necessary to achieve such perfection. To subsequently watch a poor partnership brings home just how good the harmonious pairs are. Some rounds always look untidy, for instance: The handler that has forgotten the course. The handler stuttering his way round unsure of what the dog will do next. The dog twisting in circles rather than working on. The excitable dog that barks throughout its round. The handler who shouts and screams. This is all avoidable at the basic teaching stage be it basic control or basic Agility training.

Creating a happy, quiet, fast, confident dog must be the aim. To achieve this certain training rules must be observed. Start by jumping the dog over two or three obstacles in succession. Hurdles are an obvious choice for this. If good control has been obtained this is the time to use it to good advantage for the 'Sit', 'Wait', 'Come', 'Heel', and 'Away' commands will all play a part. Run the dog at heel over the three hurdles. If all is well repeat this once or twice more. Should poles be knocked down do not worry too much at this stage. However should the dog run past any hurdle he must have several lessons on that hurdle before reverting to three in a line again. When satisfied that all is well leave the dog at the start giving a firm 'Wait' command and signal. Go to the far side of the third hurdle, turn and face the dog, pause for a second, then recall him over the obstacles. With luck the dog will jump all three without hesitation but maybe he will run out on one or more. If so recall him over each obstacle one by one several times. Rather than ask for a formal present from the dog allow him to run by or, preferably, throw his favourite toy as he takes off over the last hurdle. The direction of throw should be identical to that in which the dog is travelling with the article landing ahead of him. This will have the effect of keeping him happy whilst also being a reward for a job well done, building speed and getting the dog to go on alone. Following several successful recalls over three consecutive hurdles dog and handler should adopt the position from which he has been previously recalled. When sent on he should immediately respond by taking number one hurdle whilst the handler runs behind encouraging him on to number two. This action is repeated for the final hurdle with the play article being thrown over his head so that after landing he runs on to retrieve it. Now he can be called back with the article in his mouth. So in one quick throw so much is being achieved. Of course if the dog has not been taught to retrieve, the process of getting the article back becomes laborious. Maybe the dog has no interest in a chase. If this is so getting the dog to work on ahead becomes more difficult. With rare exceptions a dog that enjoys the thrill of the chase loves to jump on in Agility. With some dogs whose retrieve instinct is abnormally strong and the obedience a little weak jumping on can be a succession of embarrasing eliminations. The reverse, with exceptions, is also true. The dog that does not enjoy a chase may prove more difficult to be taught how to jump on. Certainly, recalls over three straight hurdles should be employed but this also applies to the retrieve happy dog. It has to be an advantage to leave the dog at the start while moving two or three obstacles ahead without expending energy. The dog can then be recalled over several obstacles while the handler starts his own run when appropriate. However should the disinterested retrieving dog be under training, those recalls can be to his food dish. In this way recalls over jumps can subsequently become sendaways over jumps to the feeding bowl.

Often three hurdles are to be found on line but the third one will constitute wrong course if taken by the dog. This will be because the subsequent part of the course requires a turn after the second hurdle, thus making hurdle number three a trap. The dog taught to work on with little control will more than likely fall into the trap. It is therefore obvious that good control is necessary. Of course should this situation arise at the start of the course the clever handler will leave the dog at the start, walk up the course to stand in front of the offending hurdle, then call the dog to him before directing him away from a possible wrong course.

BARKING AND CIRCLING

Some very keen jumpers continually bark with excitement during an Agility round. Such behaviour does not look or sound very professional particularly when handlers shout and scream instructions to the dog hoping they will be heard above his noise. At times I have been asked how to stop a dog barking. The answer is very simple yet totally frustrating for the handler with such a problem. Never let it happen in the first place then there is no problem. Immediately the dog attempts to bark in training is the time to stop it. Usually a verbal 'No' will be sufficient at this stage. If allowed to pass unchecked accompanied by praise for doing other things right, this problem will get worse. How easy it is to confuse a dog, he is a creature of habit and will therefore bark associating making a noise while jumping. How is the dog to know whether the praise was for barking, jumping or both. His association of ideas being that he was barking and his handler has approved. Those with such a problem have brought it upon their own heads or perhaps ears in this case.

There is little that can be done with a non-stop jumping barker. Being very harsh will of course mean breaking another rule, 'do not chastise on or in the vicinity of Agility equipment'. One method that has had some success is to carry a squeezy bottle of water and squirt it at his face every time he attempts to bark. If he dislikes such treatment then it can have the desired effect. Beware though of always having to carry a squeezy bottle, for some dogs learn quickly, refusing to respond when the handler is not carrying that which he has learned to dislike. If using this technique the handler must go to great lengths concealing the bottle plus catching Fido unaware of what will happen. When the dog stops barking that is the time to praise him.

Circling is another untidy problem. Dogs that jump, look back, turn and circle also create a lack of fluency in the round. It must cost many seconds for unnecessary ground covered in time wasted. Again, the time to stop this is before it develops into a habit. Usually it is unwittingly taught by the handler, often by laziness. It affects collie types of breeds most of all.

By continually sending a dog over or through an obstacle and then calling him back to the handler will develop this problem nicely. Even if the handler wishes to practise a particular obstacle ten times he would be wiser to put out at least one further obstacle for the dog to negotiate. Sending him on after the second obstacle will also help stop such an unwanted association of ideas.

Some dogs are actually taught to do this even twisting in the air whilst traversing a hurdle. I can only assume that it is in the mistaken belief that if the dog looks back after each obstacle it can then be told where to go next. It has already been made clear that there are better ways to obtain the required response. What can be better to a dogger than watching a dogging work of art? As I have said previously the aim should be fluency of movement from dog and handler working in total harmony. Dogs that circle and bark do nothing to create this impression.

COMPETITION PREPARATION

Much disappointment can be avoided if the prospective competitor realises that dogs are creatures of habit. Unless the dog has been exposed to many different examples of obstacles in varying surroundings he may make many mistakes. Sometimes such mistakes are construed as disobedience or obstinacy, when in fact the dog not having had his Agility education completed, is confused and unsure. Once the dog is jumping consistently well, at home and at the training class, the handler must make the effort to take him to as many other Agility training courses as possible. The dog that has only ever jumped through an old tyre hung from a bough of the garden apple tree will be completely baffled by a strangely coloured tyre hung from a frame in different surroundings. The command "Up" having a sensible meaning to him on his own tyre in the garden, will most likely make him question his handler's sanity when it is given in front of strange equipment. This problem is soon overcome by teaching the dog that the Agility command must have the same association of habit when used in conjunction with similar equipment. To achieve this is only a question of giving the dog sufficient practice on strange equipment, for doing so will give him the necessary varied experience.

If the dog has been trained on a well constructed solid dog walk or see-saw, then at his first competition encounters such obstacles that move or wobble as he traverses them, he is entitled to feel apprehensive. If such a dog is anything less than bold this could be the start of apprehension always being apparent when asked to ascend these obstacles. Once it is in the dogs mind to worry on an obstacle it becomes a long job to alter the condition. It is far better to initially train him on reasonably solid equipment then carefully introduce him to less sound obstacles in the controlled environment of the training class. In this way when suddenly asked to ascend rickety equipment at a show it becomes unlikely that any long term fear of such obstacles will set in.

Any opportunity should be taken to vary the training, assuming that the handler has ensured it is safe to do so. During competition one piece of equipment that has caught many inexperienced Agility handlers is the collapsible tunnel. The dog has probably quickly learned to master his own tunnel in the first place so it is easy to make the mistake of assuming that he will tackle any collapsible tunnel he comes across. The opposite is often the case, with the dog either failing to recognise that it is a tunnel and therefore running by, or else putting his head into the entrance then refusing to go any further because it is dark. For the inexperienced Agility dog a variation of different types of tunnel is most important. This will enable him to learn that all tunnels are to be fearlessly passed through.

The careful handler will also take the opportunity to ensure that a variety of colours and styles of obstacles have been jumped by the dog prior to competition. Variety must certainly be the spice of the new Agility dogs life so that strange equipment within the framework of the rules will not worry him.

Too much concentration of jumping complete courses is not a good preparation for competition. While speed is required, it must never be at the expense of control which is even more important for the potential jump-happy type of dog. With such an animal it might be better to concentrate on control by running towards an obstacle and then either calling him away or instantly dropping him.

It is always good practise to run round a training course together with the dog completely free while not allowing him to attempt jumping any obstacles. A second run may allow the dog to traverse a few obstacles the handler selects. Should the dog appear to be taking the decision to jump without instructions to do so then he must be called away from the particular obstacle that has taken his fancy. The dogs behaviour will dictate whether the third run should include traversing all, some or none of the obstacles. It is up to the handler or instructor to make the right decision according to the dogs reactions so far.

With some dogs too much repetitious jumping will only bring on boredom so the handler must be aware when to stop. When practising with the dog, as a rule of thumb guide if in doubt whether to continue or not, stop.

It is up to the instructor or handler to make the right decision for a book cannot judge what is exactly right for each dog. This is where a good dog trainer becomes apparent. One who given the necessary knowledge instinctively knows what will be right for the particular dog under training. Only three ingredients make a good trainer. The right handler, with the right information, with the right dog. With just one ingredient wrong the partnership of dog and handler will not be destined for the top.

Not every competition provides facilities for just one or two practice jumps. If the handler feels that the dog needs a practice just before the round it might be to their advantage to take with them a light portable jump that fits easily into the car.

There are many other small points that should be taken into consideration, such as exercising the dog prior to the round so that he is not uncomfortable when competing. Water for the dog will certainly be needed, and if it is likely to be a long day his food must be considered. The handler will require shoes that will give a good grip on the surface the competition is to be held on, and attention to clothing should not go amiss. Some handlers have made it a practise to wear track suits which are much smarter than many modes of dress used by dog handlers. For a team event clubs often dress their handlers in a uniform which looks smart and this approach should be encouraged. The choice of dress is usually the handlers own concern, but when competing in front of a large crowd it is better if they look the part.

5

The Training Class

The first question that potential enthusiasts must settle is the feasibility of Agility classes. The most likely possibility is that some members of a dog training club will wish to add this training to the clubs activities. If the enthusiasts are already leading committee members, one by one the problems associated with starting jumping training will be solved. If not it will probably be prudent for the group of enthusiasts to try and solve some of the problems so that an outline plan can be put forward. If the enthusiasm is only sufficient to ask someone else to solve all the problems, then perhaps a little soul searching is better conducted before going any further. Of course from a hard core of enthusiasts a new training group can be established. If there is a person amongst them who has a sufficiently large enough piece of land available then a major problem is solved. Large enough is ideally going to mean at least double the minimum size of 30×40 yds that the Kennel Club stipulates for competition. Such room is necessary, for not only will the precise course need to be laid out, but there may also be a requirement for additional learner obstacles. Also when not working, dogs and handlers will need a place to rest.

Sufficient car parking space must also be considered, for as we live in the age of the motor car, 20 dogs could mean 20 cars. Ground owned by local authorities is a possibility but the most likely answer to the land problem is farmland. In cases where the public or cattle have access to the land to be used, storage of the equipment must be taken into account. A suitable indoor venue may be found, but the size of area required makes it unlikely that church or village halls would be large enough. Old aircraft hangers and indoor riding schools offer possible venues, but the hiring fee will play a large part in the decision.

The provision of the obstacles will be the other big problem, for the cost of them can be relatively cheap or horrendously expensive. If an existing club is to commence Agility training then it is probable that among the members will be found people with sufficient skills to build them. Those who do not have such skills may be able to contribute if they have contacts for materials that can be supplied at a reasonable price. To ask professional welders and carpenters to build the whole set would make the acquisition of equipment beyond the price most clubs could afford. It is therefore a question of asking members, friends, relatives and acquaintances for help so that the cost does not become unreasonable. I have known of complete sets being built for such small sums that no club treasurer would object to parting with the money. On the other hand there have been cases where an individual has paid for a full set to be made professionally.

If the cost is beyond that which the club can reasonably afford, with sufficient enthusiasm the money can be found by various fund raising activities. It all depends on how keen any group are to get going. Maybe the main committee of a dog club will advance the money, for once several handlers have reasonably experienced dogs a demonstration team can be set up. Finances can be raised in this way for there are Agility Clubs receiving reasonable fees for demonstrations with much of the monies received being donated to charity. It really does depend on the drive and enthusiasm of the people who wish to become involved, for nothing is difficult to those with determination. Just as some people will claim that it is impossible to allocate five minutes a day to basic dog training others will claim it an impossibility to obtain land or equipment.

Once training has commenced it will become apparent that certain pieces of learner equipment can be used to great advantage. The chapter on equipment training mainly discussed full size obstacles, but the experienced dog training instructor will quickly recognise types of dog who would initially react more favourably on less imposing obstacles. The two hardboard doors hinged together to simulate a small scale will have its uses. Also the odd 9″ scaffold plank that can be raised on bricks will be useful for some learners. The newcomer spends far longer on each piece of equipment than the handler of the experienced dog who may only require one attempt at each jump, so one or two additional learner hurdles are a good idea.

Of additional help is a separate learner hoop, for there is nothing quite so frustrating at a training session than finding the hoop height different to that which ones own dog is used to. If two hoops are available then one can be left at a maximum height and the other used for height variations. Weaving poles set aside for initial teaching will prove valuable, particularly if they are of the shorter variety that allows the handler to manipulate the lead over the top of the poles.

If most of the equipment can be left erected on the training ground so much the better, and as long as it is painted or treated once a year it should not deteriorate too quickly. The winter months will of course hasten decay, so storing until the spring is always advisable. The collapsible tunnel, being made of canvas or cloth, should not be left out at all and each time that it becomes damp the material will need to be dried.

Unfortunately most clubs will probably have to erect and dismantle their obstacles at each training session and this will involve some heavy or bulky lifting. It goes without saying that such a laborious task can be made quite simple if everyone gives a hand. It is human nature for some people to avoid helping, standing idly by while others do their share of the work. The average scale jump fully erected is quite easily moved by two people. The easiest way is for two males to stand under it and take the weight of each ramp on their backs. If the lifting, erecting and dismantling of equipment is left to just a few people, it is very unfair and likely to lead to everyone standing back hoping that someone else will do it. It is more sensible for a rule to be made that all attending Agility classes must help with this work.

A decision has to be made of whether basic control is to be part of the instruction. In my opinion it is better kept quite separate from Agility training, for there is always the temptation for the handler to have a go at the jumps prior to basic control being achieved. Additionally there is the risk that the dog will associate control correction with jumping, and this might have the effect of lowering his tail. If Agility instruction is to be part of the activities of an existing dog training club, then handlers whose dogs are not yet under control should attend the requisite obedience class first. Groups training for Agility only can also recommend that dogs not sufficiently under control should first attend a club that has classes for basic obedience. This inevitably leads to the question that someone has to have the responsibility of deciding whether or not a dog is suitable for Agility training. It is not just a question of the prospective dog being under control, as other factors must also be considered. Obviously the size of the dog must be taken into account, but it is surprising how easily some smaller dogs are able to negotiate the equipment. The 6' vertical scale that requires the dog to reach the top with his paws in one leap precludes breeds that do not have the physical ability. But the fact that the Agility scale is a ramp to be run up and down by the dog makes a lot of difference. Hereditary defects such as Hip Dysplasia must be taken into account, ensuring that no dog is asked to do what his joints are not suitable for. There will be handlers who arrive with dogs very much overweight. While they can be given elementary jumping lessons they should be told quite firmly that before the dog can be allowed to attempt the full heights he must lose weight. A combination of dieting and more exercise will be the answer, but perhaps this may also apply to some of the handlers!

The instructors must ensure that the equipment is of stable construction and therefore safe for the dog. The table will need a treaded rubber mat or piece of carpet affixed to the top to ensure that the dog that lands at speed is able to stop. It will also be necessary to stake some of the equipment to the ground. The table is a classic example, for if left unstaked a fast heavy dog can cause it to tip. The frame of the see-saw usually needs secure staking to stop a bouncing effect when the down side hits the ground, and the rigidity of all equipment must be satisfactory before allowing dogs to use it.

Each new handler should have the right training equipment and those who arrive incorrectly equipped must be educated in this respect. While each dog should have a training collar it cannot be considered as the right equipment for Agility training. It is preferable, indeed to some extent essential, that the dog should be taught to jump wearing a plain collar. The danger with the check chain being that it is possible for the dog to get caught up on the jumping equipment and also for inexperienced handlers to use it incorrectly. A good example is the dog being led over the 4' 6" high dog walk for the first time, falling off and being hung by the check chain. Even experienced Agility dogs are prone to danger from the equipment if wearing a loose check chain. The next essential piece of training equipment is a strong leather or nylon lead of at least 3' 6" in length. It should have a well stitched handle and a good quality trigger hook.

Finally the handlers footwear needs some consideration, for the type of footwear people will arrive in could be quite unsuitable. A pair of training shoes are the most ideal but not essential as long as the footwear being used is not clumsy and will allow the handler to turn quickly while running.

In the initial stages it may be that there are less than 20 handlers taking part. If the class is being held over a period of one or two hours it should be impossible for a dog to be under obstacle training the whole time. Indeed the instructor must ensure that each dog is given adequate rest periods so that he is not overtaxed. Thus it is unlikely that there will be more than ten dogs using the equipment at any given time. Such a number is probably sufficient, and if the membership for Agility becomes greater it would be necessary to arrange the classes according to ability. These classes could be of approximately one hour's duration, for more time than this is an unnecessary luxury for the handler and will probably be too much for the dog.

A certain amount of discipline is always necessary at a dog training class no matter what the subject. With Agility classes it is best to adhere to certain principles so that chaos does not develop. If the club has experienced handlers, during the initial part of the training session, they can be allowed to practise on the equipment without close supervision. This can be called "Group 1". While they are practising the instructor can divide the remainder into two further groups. For instance the still inexperienced who require help could make up "Group 2" whilst those totally new to Agility would become "Group 3".

It must of course be remembered that whilst "Group 3" will require the greatest amount of attention, "Group 2" will still need to be closely studied, with advice being given wherever necessary. In most cases "Group 1" can be left to their own devices unless a handler has requested help for a problem that has recently developed.

The instructor should impress upon the newcomers that everything they do while teaching their dog on the equipment is all about giving him confidence. At the initial stages such confidence is vitally important. Sometimes it is necessary to give the handler confidence that their dog can do it. But starting with hurdle training the instructor will soon learn how much confidence and control the handler really has.

Always remember to introduce Weaving Pole training at the first session. It can be explained that this obstacle requires much longer to perfect than others and much practise will be needed.

The instructor should never assume that the handlers know how to use praise. Strangely enough many experienced handlers are inept on this subject. The dog needs to know when he has pleased his handler and in these circumstances praise should be immediate. A split second after immediate is too late. As a general guide remember the following rules:

1. Praise the dog while he is doing that which is required.
2. Beware of the handler that uses praise indiscriminately.
3. Watch out for the over-use of praise.
4. Praise incorrectly used is counter productive.

Normally all dog training is based upon correction and reward. Certainly much basic training is. However, with the prospective Agility dog that has been correctly taught basic training, it is possible and indeed preferable to teach Agility without correction, the use of correctly timed praise being sufficient.

Of assistance to the newcomers is some of the experienced dogs and handlers demonstrating complete rounds. This gives them the idea of what they should try and achieve or if possible better. For the experienced it is better that they are asked what problems they have with likely cures being considered. Beware those new to instructing at dog training classes for inevitably you will be told "I have tried that and it doesn't work". What is usually meant is that they tried it once or twice without magical success so they gave up. When suggesting alternative methods the answer will probably be the same with this type of handler. For me continual suggestions would be a waste of breath. With fools I have little patience, but dogs are rarely fools and are worthy of all my patience.

Each handler new to Agility should have a certain amount of individual instruction on each piece of equipment. They should never be allowed to 'have a go' without being shown the logical teaching progression on each obstacle. If they do it is likely that basic mistakes will be made which will later prove difficult to eradicate. The instructor should start them off on hurdles so that the dog learns to understand what is required when the jumping command is used. Once this has been learned the dog can be introduced to the table, 'A' Ramp, dog walk, brush jump and tyre all with the same command. While all the equipment can be taught using one command, the use of "Up" may sound peculiar when applied to tunnels and weaving poles, so an additional command can be used. Certainly personal instruction on each item is the only way to minimise training mistakes.

Having given each new dog the basic hurdle training instruction they are best paired with someone of the same standard so that they can operate together. It is impossible for one or even two instructors to be everywhere at once, so when the learner pupils are paired the explanation only has to be given once before subsequently leaving the two handlers to assist each other. The reader will recall that teaching the 'A' Ramp, dog walk, table and tunnels is often a two person operation. While personal help can be given to each pair it is unlikely that any instructor of a busy class would be able to be with them the whole time. It is therefore preferable for the instructor to show both pupils how to proceed with their dogs before leaving them to assist each other so that he is free to help others. Of course the instructor should periodically return to assess the progress, for in such a way it is possible that the equipment and available time will be fully utilised.

With so many handlers and dogs of various abilities using the equipment it is essential that chaos does not develop. It is probable that the equipment has been built as a course to be used by the more experienced dogs. If this is so, the instructor should make quite clear the order and direction in which each jump should be traversed. Once established no handler should be permitted to jump a dog over an obstacle the opposite way to the course direction. There is a great temptation for inexperienced handlers to allow or even encourage their dogs to jump back and forth over the obstacles. Often it is just a case of the handler being lazy. More worrying is the handler who stands back in pleasant surprise as his dog volunteers to return over the jump. Such practices should be stopped at the outset for it is all too easy to erroneously teach the dog to return over an obstacle having first traversed it in the correct direction. If not a habit could soon develop which might later manifest itself in the competition arena. With the collapsible tunnel it is of course impossible, but most other pieces can be traversed either way. This might lead to two dogs scaling simultaneously from either side only to meet at the apex. Similar problems arise when dogs meet on the walk with one either being told to jump off or worse still doing so without command.

Neither case will assist with the dogs training for the dog must not be allowed to leave the equipment until the extremity has been reached.

One of the great advantages of Agility training is that many dogs that already respond to basic control can be taken over or through most obstacles at their first supervised training session. This will not usually include the see-saw for reasons to be explained hitherto, and in most cases the dog will be on the lead. A bold dog carefully handled can at the first session traverse most obstacles, which will give him variety and the handler hope. The reader should not misinterpret this as meaning that a dog can be trained in one hour. Far from it, but certainly dogs with good basic control can learn to jump happily before their handlers have had time to nag and bore them. Such an initial approach is not to be confused with the handler who, without sufficient obstacle training or basic control, attempts a complete course run with the dog on a lead. This is never a good approach as it is far better for the handler to teach the dog to be able to consecutively jump three or four obstacles without lead assistance than to charge round the whole course with the dog on a lead. Even the handler of the experienced dog must be wary, for practising complete courses has a certain value dependent upon the dogs experience and attitude to jumping. As soon as an experienced dog has been round a new course once he will tackle it more easily a second time. If he has further attempts at the same course it is very easy for the unsuspecting handler to think that the dog is improving quickly. What he is really doing is working from memory rather than learning to be handled on a strange course, which is what will eventually be necessary.

It has already been mentioned that the use of tit-bits for teaching purposes is quite permissible. However inconsiderate handlers may leave particles of food on the equipment thus giving problems to the handler of a greedy dog that follows. The instructor must ensure that any tit-bits used are not of the variety that might leave crumbs or traces, as the use of food being an aid to one handler can be a nuisance to another.

Once the training class has one or two dogs that have mastered all the obstacles lead free, they can become members of "Group 1". No doubt they will wish to practise at least one complete course to improve their own handling techniques. The only way to do this is to set aside a time for the better dogs to have their practise. When just a few dogs are at this level of competancy perhaps two 10 minute sessions will suffice. It is important that handlers whose dogs make a mistake during one of these practise rounds do not stop to re-train on the particular piece of equipment on which the dog faulted. Any re-training must be done during the general session, for no handler attempting a full round should be on the course for more than approximately one minute. If each handler attempting a full course is allowed to re-train they could each monopolise all the equipment for ten minutes. It can be advantageous if the course is cleared for full round attempts at the beginning of a training session. Providing that each week the layout is altered before the handler has had a chance to practise one or two pieces during a general session, a complete run enables the handler to assess progress on untried courses. This is as near as they will get to competition conditions which rightly do not allow handlers to practise the course, and is another reason why it is so important that the training course is always altered. The dogs will not learn to rely on instructions from their handlers if they are allowed to complete training courses by memory.

The instructor should always be watching the better dogs attempt a full course so that advice can be given on tactical handling. As discussed in Chapter 4, precious seconds can be saved by skilful handling and the instructor must always be able to offer constructive advice.

Sometimes team competitions are arranged, so being aware of the better dogs in the class enables the instructor to select the most suitable team. Needless to say the club should make an effort to dress the team in a uniform rather than allowing individuals to dress as they wish. Printed 'T' shirts and track suits are the obvious answer to the problem, but unless the club is paying for the purchase, the financial circumstances of the team members must be taken into consideration.

One very important aspect of an organised training class is keeping the land clean. If adequate rough exercising areas are not available then someone must take the responsibility of ensuring abnoxious deposits are not left for others to find.

6

Avoiding or Solving Problems

Most agility problems can be traced back to insufficient basic training or incorrect application. In some cases the problem has been caused by a lack of conditioning for a specific situation. Such situations may be commonplace at the Agility event or even less obscure. Of course the bold dog usually takes all these things in his stride and if a suitable breed for Agility he could be the ideal material.

Not everyone is fortunate enough to have perfect material to work with. They may well have one of the breeds that more frequently win prizes than others but theirs is not so suitable. Then there are apparently suitable dogs whose handlers come across what appears to be an insurmountable problem. Far be it for me to suggest that every problem can always be eliminated. That is not the way training dogs works out and I would not be telling the truth if I gave the impression that this book or my instruction can solve all problems. Many yes, but there are those solutions that have eluded me during my dog training life so I am sure there are more to come. The day I decide that I know all the answers will be the day to quit. However some problems I have encountered with my own or other handlers dogs do have solutions. Remember though that your dog might just require that different approach.

Many problems only become apparent when the dog starts competition. For instance there are dogs that will react totally differently on the competition course to the way they do in training. These types make life very difficult for their handlers or instructors as in many ways they can be described as having become ring crafty. Generally the only recourse is for the handler to try simulating show conditions in training. This is where other class members can assist by trying to create the right atmosphere that will enable appropriate action to be taken.

There is the strong willed dog whose handler probably paid insufficient attention to basic training before proceeding with Agility. While training at the usual club venue the dog may never repeat mistakes frequently made in competition. For example I have known a dog that can miss at least two out of three contacts in most competition classes entered. When it comes to correcting the errors in training the dog makes each contact perfectly. This particular dog would start barking while nearing a contact area as though arguing with the handlers vocal and signalled instructions. Such commands having been worked upon during normal training sessions. In this instance the barking would never have commenced in the first place if basic training principles had been followed. However, just telling a handler they got it all wrong when they started is not really sufficient. Some action can prove successful once the real problem has been analysed. Obviously the dog, being a creature of habit, knows that his behaviour is unacceptable at training classes but also knows that his handler will do little about it in competition. One answer is to simulate competition conditions in training. To do so requires the co-operation of other club members so that similar situations can be set up. If one understands why certain dogs will always bark when the telephone rings we are half way to creating a competition environment. Usually it is because, from the moment the dog was introduced to his home, each time he heard ringing, excitement was engendered by the humans rushing to answer it. Such conditions often apply in a house that has excitable teenagers. If they had been taught to walk calmly to the telephone it is odds on the dog would not react in the way he does. For our purpose with Agility training this tells us that a lot of excitement with dogs working to commands being given will generally do the trick. One way is by using all the clubs competition dogs in a relay over a normal type of course with a baton change on the start/finish line. The last dog to go will be the offender who, in all probability, will react in a similar manner to competition by repeating his mistakes. The handler must not waste this opportunity to correct him by the instructors prescribed manner. It is impossible by book to suggest what form of correction should be used. It really depends on the dog, his nature and temperament, with only those sufficiently experienced being likely to find the right balance. A gentle 'No' for instance might be right for one, with much rougher handling having little effect on another.

A similar way of producing the excitement engendered during competition is for another dog and handler to chase the offender around the course starting one or two obstacles behind. This is also useful for the dog that is a little course shy or maybe worries about a particular obstacle. With this type shyness or worry should not be confused with boredom, for excitement brought about by the chase will be sufficient stimulus for the dog to also respond in an excited manner. Such excitement can become pleasure for the dog thus what was a problem has been overcome.

Another handler working the dog up at the start can speed up a lethargic animal be he shy or bored, or even inject a little more speed into an already speedy dog. This is done by the usual handler standing near to the starting line while a friend teases the dog attempting to excite him about rejoining his handler. At the last minute the dog is returned to his handler with a faster round being a possible result.

Playing with the dog immediately prior to competition can also help to combat lethargy howsoever induced in the first place. Maybe play retrieves are sufficient for the dog who becomes excited with such games. For another playing tug on an old sock can work wonders. However, no matter how precisely this last minute competition preparation is timed there will be occasions when just as you thought it was your turn a further period of waiting becomes necessary. Frustrating yes, but a regular competitor will become used to such occurrences.

If, despite all remedial action having been unsuccessful, all the old problems remain there is a further course of action that can be taken. Using another experienced handler to train and/or compete with your dog can sometimes break the offending pattern that is so ingrained into this ring crafty creature of habit. Needless to say such a handler must know exactly what they are doing to have any chance of changing behavioural patterns before the dog recreates them.

The vast majority of course problems have an answer. Talk to the experienced, explain the problem precisely, then listen carefully to the suggested answers.

OBSTACLE PROBLEMS

WING JUMPING

Some Agility dogs are more prone to jumping hurdle wings than others. Often the equipment is at fault for it is my view that there should always be a distinct difference between the wing and the hurdle itself. The side support of the wing that will hold the jumping bar should always be six to twelve inches higher than the top part of the wing's slope. With such equipment it is unusual for the dog to make a mistake. Only the inexperienced partnership will do so, particularly when the handler runs wide of the hurdle thus encouraging the dog to move towards his handler rather than traverse the centre of the obstacle.

BANKING

Banking is a term used in horse jumping circles. It also adequately describes using the feet, or paws, or part of the obstacle as assistance to traverse it. It is generally only inexperienced dogs that will do this. Obviously obstacles such as walls become more inviting for the dog to make such attempts. Bearing in mind that dogs dislike climbing upon anything that wobbles, making the top of likely obstacles unstable and prone to collapse will cure such problems.

KNOCK DOWNS

A common problem particularly for the dog lacking height or length of leg. Sometimes this can be attributed to the dog mis-timing his take off, usually commencing to rise too soon rather than too late. With the less bold types, as they progressively knock poles down they may stand off even further in the mistaken belief that doing so will solve the problem. With this type it is really a case of practise makes perfect encouraging them to lift off at the right time by being alongside.

If the handler is sure it is just a question of the dog being lazy and he is of a bold enough nature not to be easily disturbed, then a heavily weighted hurdle pole can be used. For safety it must be affixed so that as his knuckles are rapped it falls easily. After one or two such episodes the discomfort should ensure that in future he lifts his legs higher. In all but the most stubborn cases such treatment should be sufficient. Taking matters one step forward a piece of tin placed on the ground where the weighted pole is to fall will have the added effect of sudden noise. Beware, this is only for the bold and those not gun shy. With some, one clatter will be sufficient to cause a fear of noise which is not the desired result. Only the very experienced trainers can gauge the likely response to given circumstances and sometimes they can get it wrong. One certainty is that this book cannot give the perfect answer, as the handler or his instructors must be responsible for such decisions.

SPREAD JUMPS

Of course some hurdles, particularly spread jumps, can convey a confusing image to the dog. We all know that the eyesight of the dog is not nearly as powerful as that of humans, but both species have differing degrees of sight. With dogs basically being colour blind, in the case of a spread that has units of differing colours on the front and back some dogs may see it as one. If the dogs eyes only detect one unit his leap will be mis-timed, therefore knockdowns will result.

There are handlers who use a different hurdle command when it comes to spread jumps, delivering such a command in a more urgent manner. By doing so their aim is to convey to the dog that this hurdle requires a bigger leap than others. This approach has some merit but to clutter the dogs vocabulary with too many commands leaves him with a lot to remember. A more urgent use of the normal command will often suffice and convey the requisite message.

Sometimes the handler is his own worse enemy instructing the dog to jump before he has reached the right position. If owning a dog that consistently knocks the poles down check that it is not a handler problem by saying nothing. It is possible for the handler to interfere too much rather than allow the dog to sort it out for himself. During training allowing him to make the decisions for a while may cure the problem while also teaching where his correct take off point is.

CONTACT PROBLEMS

Ask one hundred Agility handlers what their greatest problem is the majority will probably reply "contacts". Those yellow or different coloured areas have at times reduced strong men to tears, for frustration can be the name of the game. Dogs start their competitive Agility careers with different standards of expertise. Some handlers, particularly badly advised beginners, enter their dog in competition even though he has never made a contact in training. Initially such a dog has little or no chance of success in the ring and probably will continue to miss the vast majority throughout his competition life. Other better instructed handlers will commence competition with a dog that makes every contact, but as time goes on the occasional missed one becomes a much more frequent occurrence. Generally speaking speedy dogs, particularly those who become progressively excited, are more prone to such problems than their slower cousins.

So what can be done to combat the dogs natural inclination to jump on or off rather than walk up and down almost the whole length? In the first place it stands to reason that the dog should never be allowed to miss a contact right from the beginning. As already mentioned such practise is not going to guarantee permanent success, but it will certainly give him a better idea that this is what is wanted. Some dogs, in their enthusiasm to please, will start by leaping on to the obstacle thereby missing the "Up" contact. Usually this habit disappears with experience but, if persistent, must be changed. When the dog has been given thorough basic training he will have a fast responsive immediate down. Therefore just before he commences his leap he can be dropped momentarily, followed by a controlled ascent on to the contact. Alternatively a tyre, the same size as that used for Agility, can be placed at the bottom of the dog walk or ramp with the dog being required to go through it prior to ascending. This will ensure that he cannot avoid touching the contact so that after many sessions his habit of starting too high has been changed.

So much for ascent, but most problems occur on the down side. Similar to using a tyre at the bottom of the 'A' Ramp, hoops can be made the same diameter as the tyre opening and used at the bottom of the up and down sides of all contacts. The idea will be for the dog to consistently pass through these hoops in training which, by doing so ensures that he does not miss contacts. Used to combat an already ingrained pattern of missing contacts this solution will help some dogs but do little for others. A higher degree of success can be obtained from the dog whose initial training on all contact area obstacles includes the use of hoops. In such cases one positive result is being achieved. The dog is not being allowed to form the habit of missing contacts. There is also the possibility that, if consistently used in training over a long period of time, habit dictates that he will learn to start and finish the obstacles by stepping on most of the contacts.

One type of dog will decide he is in a race to the end of the obstacle. This becomes apparent when the more the handler tries to get to the

end before the dog, the faster he goes, thus continuing to leap off
from too great a height. When this problem manifests itself the dog
can usually be slowed down if the handler ceases the race by hanging
back. It often has the effect of making the dog wait for his handler.
Combine this with appropriate firm commands and sanity can be
restored. However it can cause additional handling problems
because of an inability to resume position beside or in front of the
dog before he alights.

If the handler has the ability to be beside or in front of the dog as
he descends then remedial action will be less of a problem. One
method that has success is to press the dog on to the contact by using
a flat hand that applies sufficient pressure upon his neck. This is
commenced before the point that he usually leaves from and continues until satisfied that he is low enough to be allowed to leave. Of
course commands such as "Steady" should be used simultaneously.
One thing experienced dog trainers are well aware of is that teaching
the dog remedies for one problem can develop another. Here we
have a classic case for the dog may well associate the arm movement
as a signal to get off. To avoid this the arm must travel at the speed of
a striking Cobra, being brought up in front of the dogs nose, then
above his neck. Providing this method is consistently applied whilst
training, in competition the handler has the perfect signal. Of course
the hand no longer touches the dog who is not to know that it will not
do so. The signal should be reinforced with the appropriate
command which will remind the dog to stay on the contact.

Titbits can be used to advantage but please not just as a general
reward. This mistaken use usually follows a delay while the
container is found from a pocket with further delay while it is
opened. By the time the dog is lucky he has forgotten why he is being
rewarded. A better way is to hold a small titbit in the hand furthest
from the obstacle. As the dog is descending, but still a minimum of
half a metre or a yard away, the hand containing the titbit hidden
amongst fingertips is brought in front of his nose. In much the same
fashion as a carrot in front of the donkey, the hand draws the dog
down and well on to the contact before he is, quickly and without
fuss, allowed to take the reward.

Alternatively, the hand containing a titbit is held very low down
on the contact inviting the dog to come to it. Which of these two
methods will suit the dog under training is for the handler to decide.
It might even be neither for some dogs can become very crafty when

given food in training. Used skilfully titbits can be a marvellous aid but with the crafty dog the handler must remember not to give one every time he descends. By not allowing the dog to be sure whether or not he will be lucky he is unlikely to develop the habit of only working for food. With others it is better to give the titbit every time in training, the instructor or handler must decide which way is best. However, to ensure the signal is understood when competing the empty hand should still go through the same motions. What must be considered is why the dog tries to jump off early. In some cases it just happens because he decides he is near enough to the ground to jump. These types are easy to cure but unfortunately this is not generally the case. The methods described above to combat the problem are all formulated to avert the dogs eyes from obstacles ahead, for in most cases, if you can get his eyes upon the hand he has momentarily forgotten about the obstacles ahead. Thus his incentive is greater to stay on the obstacle for a reward rather than leave prematurely for the next obstacle.

Body signals are often given without the handler knowing. Maybe in their haste to depart to the next obstacle the handler is unconsciously giving signals that in effect the dog is obeying by departing immediately they are noticed. Another likely reason for premature departure is good old fashioned anticipation and this is where an immediate down can be used to effect. Of course the dog must be steadied first by vocal command and when he has covered at least half of the contact the 'Down' command is given. After a short pause he is not allowed to leap off but rather to walk a few more inches before being allowed to leave in a controlled manner. Every training method has a reason that makes it work. The down creates an extra part of the total exercise. The dog being a creature of habit learns it has not finished until the final component has been used. In this case a down followed by walking on again.

DOG WALKS AND SEE-SAWS

While all dog walks should be completely stable and rock solid, some used for competition tend to wobble. If the dog has not been accustomed to unsteady dog walks expect possible adverse reactions from all but the most bold types when they are encountered. Therefore it makes sense to ensure that less than stable walks are familiar to the dog. Do not be tempted to make the walk so unsteady that even the bold dog will become wary, but rather by proceeding with care ensure that he does not associate stress with the obstacle.

Fear of both obstacles can also be caused if the handler consistently allows a fast dog to attempt the obstacle at an angle. Invariably he will slip off which, if too frequent an occurrence, can cause an association of fear. See-saws by their very nature are unsteady so from first attempts care must be taken to ensure that stress is not induced. Making the dog pause fractionally before the tipping point will invariably achieve the desired effect. It also stops the fast dog running off into the air before tilting the plank. Once again good basics help, for an immediate down at the appropriate moment steadies the dog.

WEAVING POLES

Most problems are just a case of insufficient training and thereby lies the answer. However, there are some points to remember. For example always practise with odd and even numbers of poles so the dog is used to the exit being on either side. If he is correct but slow try getting ahead of the dog to induce speed. Alternatively bait him with food or use play retrieves as he exits. Of little comfort to those with pole problems is the fact that the fault can be traced to the original method of training. Do however remember one important point. The dog must not associate duress with the Weaving Poles.

7

Constructing Agility Equipment

One of the greatest problems facing people new to Agility is equipment construction. To have obstacles made professionally can prove to be very expensive and therefore many will wish to make their own.

The sole purpose of this chapter is to provide obstacle designs that are relatively simple to construct providing the intended manufacturer has a rudimentary knowledge of DIY or wood working techniques. The designs have been developed in consultation with my good friend Alan Clubley who has also been responsible for the excellent drawings.

When discussing obstacle design we were aware that many of those shown in the first edition of "The Agility Dog" still hold good today. However it was decided to produce new designs and drawings based upon certain principles.

With the exception of the See-Saw and Weaving Poles we have avoided the necessity of welding so that any reasonably competent handyman will be able to construct obstacles that are safe, strong, stable, easily transported in a trailer and once unloaded, quickly erected. In this connection the See-Saw is a problem for although there are pivot methods that would not require welding techniques we felt it unavoidable in this case.

To ensure safety for the dog it should go without saying that certain construction principles must be paramount. All wooden edges and corners should be rounded off and nothing must protrude that could possibly injure the dog, even in the most unlikely circumstances.

All surfaces on which the dog is required to walk should be sanded to provide a non-slip surface. This is easily accomplished by sieving dry sand onto the wet undercoat. Once dry the particles of sand that are still loose can be brushed off prior to finally painting with a top coat. A surface on which the dog can grip is the result.

Most countries have Agility measurements similar to those used in Great Britain but there may be slight differences which should be taken into account when interpreting these measurements and drawings. All drawing measurements are quoted in millimetres whereas the text shows measurements in imperial with millimetres in brackets. All timber measurements quoted are those after the wood has been finished or planed. Of further assistance may be the imperial/metric conversion table to be found on the last page of the book.

Not every dimension has been given as some will be quite apparent when studying the drawings, text and relevant Agility regulations. Sufficient information is shown which combined with common sense will produce obstacles not only safe and sturdy but also grace an Agility ring.

On the basis that a full set of equipment would include one of all the usual eight obstacles it can be seen that eight hurdle type obstacles would be the very minimum to make a set of equipment. Without using any obstacle more than once a Judge would be restricted to a sixteen obstacle course. Should a spread jump be used, one less hurdle standing alone is available. It therefore follows that between 8 & 13 hurdle type obstacles complete a set of equipment that allows the judge scope when designing his course.

Those who do not have the time or skill to make Agility equipment would do well to contact Premier Jumps who have been manufacturing such obstacles almost since the birth of Agility. Their address is:

Premier Jumps
"Triddles Farm"
Plough Road
Smallfield
Horley, Surrey
England
RH6 9JN

HURDLES

To make a quick temporary practise hurdle is very simple. All that is necessary is two uprights with five blocks attached at regular intervals to allow the training bars to be raised or lowered. With metal spikes on the bottom of the uprights they can be driven into

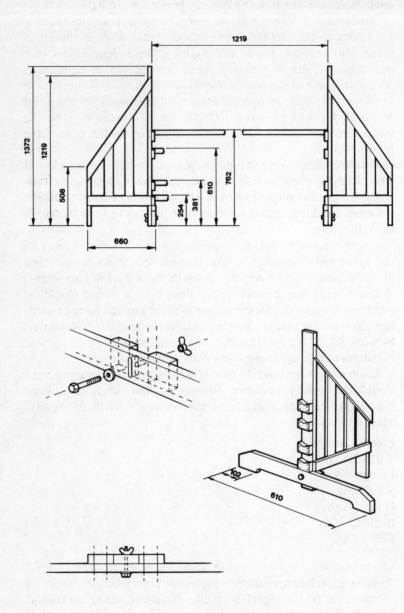

Fig. 5 Hurdles

even the hardest ground.

Hurdles with wings are more attractive for competition purposes, having the effect of making the equipment more substantial. As most competition hurdles have wings, at some time or other it becomes necessary to train the dog on winged hurdles.

The timber used in construction is 3″ × 2″ (76 × 51) for the main verticals. The cups that support the cross poles can be made from 3″ × 1″ (76 × 25) wood fixed in position that will result in pole heights being set at 10″ 15″ 24″ 30″ (254 381 610 762) respectively. These heights allow for mini competitions and for training but are best adjusted to comply with national rules.

A 1.5″ (38) pole 6′ (1829) long is suitable and can be made from wood or plastic plumbing material. However for competition purposes this latter type of pole is rather susceptable to being blown off in heavy winds and therefore some method of weighting may be necessary.

The design only requires one foot per upright which is attached to the verticle pole that supports the cross poles. The foot is made from 1″ × 7″ × 24″ (25 × 178 × 610) wood recessed underneath by 1″ (25). When secured to the pillar this recess allows the wing to stand securely on three legs. The slotted hole on the foot allows for adjustment of height if the ground is uneven. By the use of bolt and wing nut this becomes quite simple. As the foot is only held by one bolt, to ensure that the jump remains upright two blocks 2″ × 1″ (51 × 25) are fixed either side of the vertical support.

The hurdle wing dimensions described above and shown in the drawing are for competition purposes. They are a little too large for training which preferably requires a wing height not in excess of 3′ (914). This lower height allows for easier use of the lead during initial training.

TABLE

The speed at which some dogs land on the table together with the angle of their arrival means that this piece of equipment is subject to continual strain. This strain is exaggerated by the fact that it is preferable for the table to be pegged to the ground, thus avoiding the obstacle tipping over when the dog lands at speed.

The design of the 2′6″ (762) high table shown in the drawing, if carefully made, will give the requisite stability. The corner vertical posts are 3″ (76) square supported by 3″ × 1″ (76 × 25) cross struts

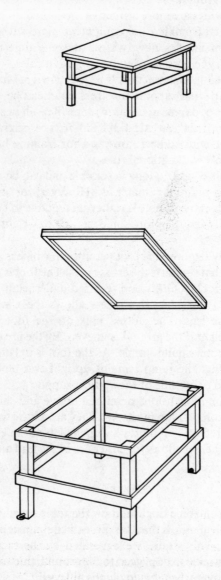

Fig. 6 Table

which are screwed to the vertical posts. The table can have hook eyes secured to two legs which allows for stakes to be driven into the ground through these eyes.

The 3' 6" (1067) square table top is constructed from 9mm exterior quality plywood and mounted on a 1" × 1" (25 × 25) wooden frame. It should be screwed to the ply from the top and suitably countersunk. Remember to ensure the table top has a non-slip surface which can be incorporated during painting as previously advised. Other methods of ensuring that the dogs do not slip are to cover the surface with rubber, carpet, or hessian.

WALL JUMP

This piece of equipment, while not being necessary for training purposes, is quite imposing and therefore graces a competition ring. It is however one of the more bulky items to transport. Comprising two separate pillars and a wall the framework is made from 1.5" (38) square timber. It may be felt that for the pillars 1" (25) square timber is sufficient.

The top part of the wall is 6" × 1" (152 × 25) timber 6' (1829) long. The height of the wall is determined by the material that is used for

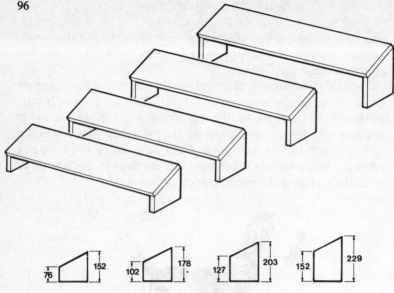

Fig. 7 Long jump

LONG JUMP

Normally three to five separate units constitute a long jump. However with British regulations stating that the overall length should not exceed 5′ (1524) it has been found that five can be too many. The drawing therefore shows four units.

Construction is very simple and 6″ × 1″ (152 × 25) timber can be used throughout. It has been designed so that each unit fits inside the other. The largest unit has a width of 4′ (1219) and the smallest 3′6″ (1067). With the other units falling between these two measurements storing and transportation is simplified.

The largest back unit is the tallest with the front unit being the smallest. The angle at which to cut the top part of the legs is 30 degrees.

To ensure rigidity a minimum of three or four screws per side should be driven through pre-drilled and countersunk holes in the top and into the legs.

If found to be necessary the design allows for corner strengthening pieces to be fitted on the under side, but the nest will not be so compact.

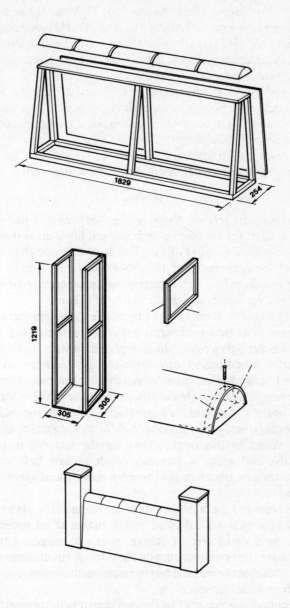

97

Fig. 8 Wall jump

the bricks or coping stones on the top. They should be loose and therefore easily knocked off by the dog. 6" (152) guttering can be used in 14.25" (362) lengths with the ends filled with a semicircle of wood. Alternatively the same ends could have hardboard covers formed round the arc.

The width of the pillars can be 12" (305) and the height 4'9" (1219). They should have a plywood base with loose caps for the top. During transportation or storage they will make a useful receptacle for smaller pieces of equipment.

To cover the framework, whilst hardboard can be used, 5 millimetre exterior grade plywood will give a longer life.

TUNNELS

The most commonly used pipe or flexible tunnel is that which is manufactured for air ducting in mines and other areas that require large temporary supplies of air. The normal diameter is 24" (610) with a minimum length of 10' (3048). In Great Britain they are usually bought in four or five metre lengths, experience showing that the latter length gives greater flexibility of shape.

The Collapsible Tunnel usually poses a few problems but all can be overcome. It is best made with a wooden entrance and material which is either lightweight canvas or plastic. Neither is perfect under all weather conditions so some explanation is necessary. In rainy or wet conditions plastic is the most suitable but generally a little heavy for the very small dogs. On the other hand while canvas is ideal in dry conditions, if it does rain the water tends to stick the top and bottom surfaces together, again making it difficult for smaller dogs. The design shown in this book allows for the material to be easily removable and whilst a club may decide to have both types, for obvious reasons, once a competition has commenced it should not be changed.

With regard to the manufacture of the material it is always a good idea to approach a local blind or sail maker in an endeavour to obtain the material free of charge. It can be suggested that they should have their name written on the sides. A circumference of 90" (2286) is ideal at the exit end but the material may have to be tapered to fit the wooden entrance.

To connect the material to the entrance a hem through which a draw-string is threaded can be incorporated. To avoid too much disturbance by the wind, the end from which the dog exits is best

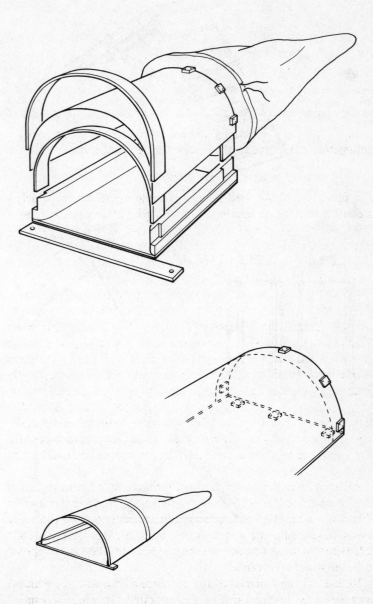

Fig. 9 Tunnels

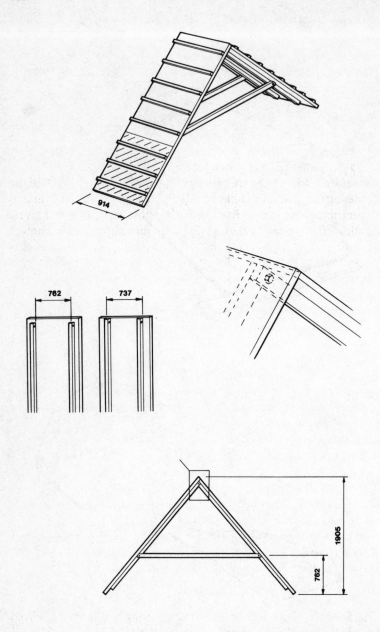

914

762   737

1905

762

Fig. 10 'A' Ramp

eyeletted in two places, 20" (208) apart, this will enable it to be staked to the ground.

The tunnel entrance is constructed on a base of 9mm exterior plywood 2' × 3' (610 × 915). Although the width is 2' (610) a 2' 6" (762) long piece of timber 3" × 1" (76 × 25) should be fixed to the front under-side so that it protrudes 3" (76) either side of the entrance. On both sides a hole should be drilled which will allow the tunnel entrance to be staked to the ground.

Along the two top sides of the baseboard should be fixed a 4" × 2" (102 × 51) timber, suitably shaped, as illustrated. This is to secure both sides of the hardboard or plywood that will form the arch of the tunnel entrance. It should have a minimum height of 19" (483) and to the entrance edge can be fixed rubber or hose pipe. This will give a cushion effect to the backs of large dogs should they make contact with the underside of the entrance. It is advisable that the entrance is strengthened by adhering a 1" (25) strip of ply or hardwood across the top and interior. At the opposite end the drawing shows 1" (25) cubes of timber spaced around the perimeter. This allows for the material draw-string to be secured tight against such blocks.

THE 'A' RAMP

The main principles to be taken into account when designing an 'A' Ramp are a compromise of portability, durability and stability. The design shown in the drawing combines all these factors.

The length of each side of an 'A' Ramp is usually 9' (2743) with a 90 degree angle at the top.

To make a robust 'A' Ramp 9 millimetre exterior grade plywood should be used for the two 9' × 3' (2743 × 914) sheets mounted on 2 vertical 3" × 1.5" (76 × 38) struts to create stability.

The design allows for eight anti-slip slats per side made from 1" × .5" (25 × 13) timber. They should be spread in such a way that no slats are within 6" (152) of the contact point which affords the judge a better view of missed contacts. The 3" × 1.5" (76 × 38) cross support shown in the drawing should be fixed to the obstacle at a height that allows the flexible tunnel to be placed underneath.

SEE-SAW

The See-Saw plank can be constructed using a standard scaffold board. In Great Britain the plank would therefore be 9" × 1.5" × 13' (229 × 38 × 3962).

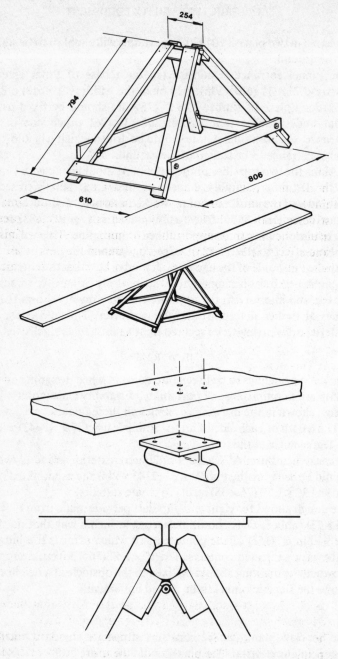

Fig. 11 See-Saw

The biggest problem with See-Saw construction is the pivot unit which will secure the plank to the base. It will usually mean that welding techniques have to be used and the design of the See-Saw shown in the drawing is no exception. An 8.5" (216) long 1.5" (38) diameter tube with .25" (6) walls or a solid bar of similar dimensions should be welded to a strip of metal 1" × .375" × 3" (25 × 10 × 76) which in turn is welded to a .25" (6) thick plate 6" (152) square. This plate should be drilled in four places so that it can be screwed, or preferably bolted, to the top plank.

The design of the base is a trestle shape and the metal tube will sit within the jaws thus providing the pivot action. The uprights are constructed from 3" × 1.5" (76 × 38) timber but the cross pieces, in particular the ones that support the pivot unit, must have a finished thickness of exactly 1" (25) as this measurement is critical. The drawing shows the tops of the trestle to be chamfered which is important to allow the plank to touch the ground at each end. Two substantial hinges are fixed to the underside of the trestle cross pieces that support the pivot as shown in the drawing.

The angle of trestle opening is controlled by 2" × 1" (51 × 25) timber which is fixed to the trestle by bolts and wing nuts on both sides. This angle can be gauged by fitting the metal pivot into the "jaws" formed by the trestles. The builder should ensure that the fit is not too loose. The maximum height should be in accordance with local regulations but in Great Britain this would not exceed 2' 6" (762).

The speed by which the plank will drop can be determined by the amount the pivot unit is offset from the centre of the plank. The first trial best being made at a 1" (25) offset from centre.

DOG WALK

The dog walk is constructed of three units 12' (3658) long. Using 9 millimetre exterior grade plywood on a 3" × 1" timber frame, rigid walkways are thus formed. An ideal width is 10" (254). Obviously national regulations will apply but those in force in Great Britain allow for a variation in width.

1" × .5" (25 × 13) wood slats can be positioned so that there are three beneath the start of the contact area and eight above.

The three 12' (3658) units are supported by two identical independent trestles. The uprights can be made from 2.5" × 1.75" (64 × 44) timber but the cross pieces do not need to be so substantial

104

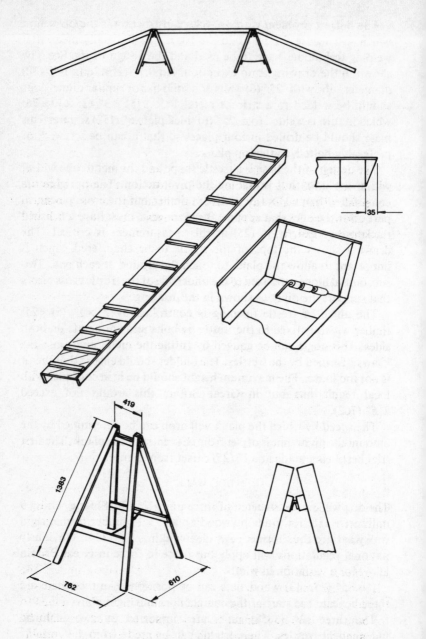

Fig. 12 Dog walk

and in this respect $2'' \times 1''$ (51×25) should be sufficient. A chain or cord should be attached to the lower cross member to ensure that the trestle does not slip apart during use.

A substantial size hinge such as a 6″ door hinge is used to secure the three units together. For storage and transportation at one end it would be feasible to leave the hinge intact. The pin from the other hinge will need to be removed and replaced with a suitably longer pin possibly attached to string so that it is not lost. This pin should not protrude in any manner which could possibly injure a dog that fell.

To strengthen the area to which the hinges are attached $8'' \times 3'' \times 3''$ ($203 \times 76 \times 76$) blocks of wood should be affixed to the underside of the walk way by screwing through from the top sides. This allows for 3″ screws to hold the hinges in position which will take the dogs weight.

HOOP OR TYRE

A hoop frame should always be built in a substantial manner. This ensures that even the largest dog is unlikely to bring the frame down on himself if jumping incorrectly. The frame should also be high enough to deter the would-be high jumper from trying to clear the whole obstacle. To be avoided and branded as dangerous are hoop jumps that comprise a tyre just screwed to two verticals.

A tyre that suits British and most countries regulations has an aperture of 16″ (406). For our purpose a Land Rover or tractor tyre can be used. The tyre can be suspended by chains attached to three substantial bolts fixed through the tread.

At least the bottom half of the tyre will need to be covered or closed to ensure that the dog cannot trap his legs when passing through. There are several methods of achieving this. One is to fill the opening with rubber or shaped wood. Another is to bind adhesive tape completely round the aperture and extremity, whilst a third method is to drill holes then sew the tyre together with plastic string as thread would not be strong enough.

The frame is constructed of $3'' \times 1.25''$ (76×32) timber sitting on base pieces made from $3.75'' \times 2.25''$ (95×57) finished timber. The width of the frame is held by a $6'' \times 1''$ (152×25) plank rebated and butted up against the vertical members which in turn are joined to the base members by a hinge. The frame is maintained vertically by two angled struts, one on either side. They are fixed to the uprights and feet by wing nuts. If two angled brackets are fitted, one in each

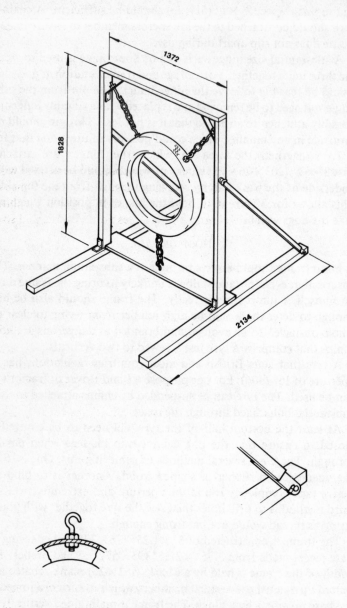

Fig. 13 Hoop or Tyre

corner of the frame, the tension of the tyre suspension can be adjusted by the use of eye bolts. The length of the chain suspending the tyre should be sufficient to allow it to be adjusted for initial training heights.

WEAVING POLES

The British Weaving Pole regulations require the pole to be not less than 30" (762) high. This is to safeguard the larger dogs catching their eyes on the top of the poles as they pass through.

For competition purposes the poles are best held in 1.5"/2" (38 × 51) diameter cups welded onto a .25" (6) metal frame having been spaced 18" (457) apart. There should be two frames containing five or six poles. Obviously it will be necessary to be able to attach the two frames together for if not the dogs will quickly move them apart.

For training purposes the above described system is too inflexible for the learner dog and easier construction methods can be used.

The quickest way is to obtain 4' (1219) broom handles before cutting them to a suitable height that allows manipulation of the lead. 6" (152) nails can be partially embedded in the bottom after drilling a pilot hole a fraction smaller than the nail.

The Weave Pole training system that I developed in the early seventies is described in chapter three. The materials for this are 3' broom handles with nails in the bottom plus string.

8

Organising Agility Competitions

When organising an Agility Test one of the first decisions that must be taken is the choice of venue. Possible venues will need to have all the usual toilet facilities, for without them life can be a little bit primitive. That consideration apart, any sports field or flat grassy area may be used, as can an indoor venue if a suitable large enough building can be found. Not only must the ring size be taken into consideration, but an additional area will also be needed for a collecting ring, plus space for the competitors to mingle when not running a dog. A further consideration for indoor venues will be the flooring medium. Sandy or peat surfaces as used by riding schools are suitable, so is concrete if it is remembered that the dog never has to land from any great height. Of far more importance than a hard landing is the degree of grip that both handler and dogs will get from the floor, as smooth slippery surfaces are entirely unsuitable.

From the beginning Agility Tests have been designed for spectator appeal and indeed the British Kennel Club regulations specifically state this. They are admirably suited to be staged in conjunction with larger events where they will probably be one of many attractions. During the summer there are innumerable agricultural shows and town or county fairs where the organisers are looking for a new attraction. Agility certainly meets such a requirement, and once convinced that it is not just another dog show, the events committee will probably welcome the idea. However, nothing is perfect so small problems may arise. It has to be remembered that such events usually rely on the monies taken at the gate to meet show expenses, and if prior arrangements have not been made with the organisers the competitors are likely to find themselves being asked to pay before being admitted. From the outset of discussions, negotiations should take place to determine what arrangements will be necessary for the competitors. At the very least each handler will require a car park pass, plus an entry ticket. If at all possible a further entry ticket should be made available for a person to act as a groom would in the horse world. This allows husband and wife entry who might not then object to paying for their children, besides there are many occasions when the handler needs someone to hold the dog, so a grooms admission ticket is to be desired.

It must be established whether there are dining facilities, either for the judge alone, or for stewards as well. The judge will expect to be fed and it is usually prudent to look after the stewards, so in the absence of suitable facilities, alternative arrangements must be made. Refreshments for the competitors and public will almost certainly be available as such ventures usually make a profit. It may be that the officials dining tickets will be issued to be used in conjunction with the general refreshments area. This is quite acceptable, the main point being that the judge and stewards are not overlooked.

An important point to establish is whether Agility will be required as one of the main ring attractions. If so it is important to ensure that the time allocated should be late enough in the day to enable an elimination contest to take place beforehand in another ring. It will be necessary for the organisers to provide a separate ring that can be used solely for Agility events throughout the day. This is where the elimination will take place, so bearing in mind the classes to be scheduled it is prudent to reserve the right to alter the order of class judging until the entry is known. Of course it makes sense that a senior Agility class should be the one to be finalised in the main arena, thus hopefully ensuring a high standard of competition. In such a case where a heat has preceded the final it is better that the final course layout is changed from that used in the heat. If ten minutes is allowed for the erection of equipment in the main arena with five minutes for its removal, a very slick arena party will be necessary. Most of the pieces can be pre-erected outside the main ring or transported fully assembled from the Agility ring. All of this saves time which will be at a premium. Certainly I have seen a well trained arena party erect and position a complete course in under five minutes, so it can be done. The Agility Club will need to insist on at least 30 minutes main arena time, and again with slick organisation, allowing half of that time for erection and knockdown, eight to ten dogs could be run. Certainly a schedule of a minute and a half or less per dog will provide fast entertainment, and entertainment is what the main arena will be all about. The longer this arena can be used for Agility the better, but whatever time is available the Agility Club will have to work out the most suitable method of filling it.

It is necessary to determine if the show committee are providing a public address system for both the Agility ring and the main arena, as it would not be prudent just to assume that this is the case. If so, and in the absence of the club possessing their own system, an additional expense will be avoided. Indeed as long as the entry fees are solely the property of the club, running an event in conjunction with a large show can be the cheapest way of promoting the sport. A large event with a captive audience is not a prerequisite for Agility Tests and indeed they can be run quite successfully on their own. However it has to be remembered that they were designed for spectator appeal so they are best suited where an audience can be found, with a public address system used for information.

The equipment for the event should be given careful thought. In the first place it must be stable and safe, but consideration should also be given to the quality. If the event is to take place in front of spectators the equipment should be smart with a professional look about it. In many instances this will be the same obstacles that the promoting club uses for training, so a week or two before the event would be the ideal time for a maintenance check to be made.

In Great Britain at least six months beforehand the club must apply to the Kennel Club for a licence to hold the event. Such applications must be made in accordance with the Kennel Club regulations which can be obtained from 1 Clarges Street, Piccadilly, London, W1Y 8AB

Countries other than Great Britain that have already established official Agility events have their own regulations and classification. The reader should therefore contact their national ruling body to determine the rules.

In Great Britain whilst Agility rules were formulated in 1980, to the date of publication they have not included a class structure, or classification as it is usually referred to.

By the time the 1983 season was drawing to a close it had become obvious that some kind of uniformity of schedule was necessary. The Agility Club was formed in November of that year as a national organisation and they recommended to their members a logical classification. In the absence of an official British Kennel Club method of determining which classes dogs are eligible for, this is the system used by the vast majority of clubs so it is reproduced below. However, as recommendations and rules have a habit of changing frequently the reader is advised to contact the Kennel Club, London, to ascertain those that are current.

AGILITY CLUB RECOMMENDED CLASSIFICATION

Agility Classes should include a minimum of two pieces of contact area equipment but should not have more than three placed in the ring.

Jumping Classes always exclude contact area equipment.

Standard Classes are Agility or Jumping Classes that have standard marking.

Novelty Classes is the general heading for classes other than standard. *eg:* Team Events, Gamblers, Snooker, Pairs, Knock-Out, Two Dog Relays, Time Gamble, or other non-standard classes as defined in a show schedule.

STANDARD CLASSES

1. **Starters** – only open to owners, handlers or dogs who have not won a first prize in a Starters, Novice, Intermediate, Open or Senior Agility/Jumping class at a licenced Agility show.

2. **Novice** – only open to dogs who have not won a total of two first prizes in Novice, Intermediate, Open or Senior Agility/Jumping classes at a licenced Agility show.

3. **Intermediate** – only open to dogs who are not eligible for Starters.

4. **Open** – open to all.

5. **Senior** – only open to dogs who have won a total of two first prizes in Novice, Intermediate, Open or SeniorAgility/Jumping classes at a licenced Agility show.

A club may schedule any or all of the above classes.

ENTRY ELIGIBILITY

All wins in standard Agility or Jumping classes should be added together and counted up to and including the seventh day before the date of closing entries. Only wins in standard classes count towards a dog's eligibility of entry. Wins in Novelty classes do not count, but such classes may be prefixed as Starter, Novice, Intermediate, Open or Senior and therefore eligibility of entry may be restricted as in 1,2,3,4,5 above.

INVITATION EVENTS

These are events by invitation only and include all competitions where dogs have previously qualified to be invited. Wins at invitation events do not count towards eligibility of entry.

This classification gives show organisers tremendous flexibility for both Agility and Jumping classes can be prefixed by Starters, Novice, Intermediate, Open or Senior. Furthermore all the Novelty classes can be prefixed in the same manner. Obviously it would be something of an impossibility to schedule all the possible permutations at one event but the very nature of the classification allows freedom of choice.

AGILITY AND JUMPING CLASSES

Known as standard classes they are the backbone of the sport being the only events in the early days. They are marked in units of five faults for each mistake plus time faults if the time set by the Judge is exceeded. These are the classes most people connect with the sport of Agility and standard marking applies.

TEAM EVENTS

Team events can be for any number of dogs with the most common being four dogs and handlers. In Great Britain the most well known team event is for clubs, with elimination events throughout the year, culminating in a final at Crufts Dog Show. This event has four dogs each starting in their own time. The result is obtained by adding the four dogs faults together. In the event of a tie the total time is taken into account.

Such events can also be run in the form of a relay with a baton change on the start/finish line. Standard marking usually applies to all types of team competitions.

PAIRS

As the title suggests a pairs class is for two dogs and handlers. Very often it is used in conjunction with a Knock Out event and can include a baton change. Standard marking usually applies with both dogs time and faults being added together to obtain the result.

KNOCK-OUT

As the name implies this class is based on the tennis type Knock-Out system of arriving at a winner. Normally it is over a jumping course which makes it very fast and exciting. It does require two identical courses with dogs competing against each other at the same time. The winners progress through to the next round until the final two run to decide who wins. As already mentioned some Knock-Out classes are run as pairs events so in effect there are four dogs in the ring at one time. Standard marking usually applies.

TWO DOG RELAYS (PAIRS)

This has a very descriptive title for two dogs and handlers are required with a baton change between handlers as the first dog finishes. Total faults and total time are taken into account to find the winning two dogs. Standard marking usually applies.

TIME GAMBLE

A time is decided by the judge which will be declared prior to the start or kept secret. Time faults are added to two decimal places for finishing with a time over or under that which has been decided by the judge. The gamble is to attempt to finish exactly on the time set by the judge. Standard marking usually applies.

HANDICAP

This class can be either Jumping or Agility and, whilst being faulted in the normal way, up to four different starting positions are decided upon. The least experienced starts at scratch with the experts having a handicap distance of maybe thirty yards/metres. This allows for other standards of dogs to start at distances in between. Standard marking usually applies.

GAMBLERS

One of the first Novelty events to be introduced to Agility. A time is set by the judge who will have decided a value for each piece of equipment which can be negotiated a maximum of twice in any direction. The values are usually three, two, one according to the degree of difficulty of the obstacle. Very often an additional five or ten seconds are added after the initial period of time. This is to enable the handler to gamble on what is usually referred to as a joker. It can consist of two or more obstacles that only score if completed within the extra time. A Gamblers Class is always an Agility course.

SNOOKER

Based upon the game of snooker there are eight or nine hurdles. Three are red with a value of one each with the rest being the same colour and value as snooker balls. They are positioned in the same manner as the game of snooker with often a See-Saw being used as the black. Dogs attempt each red hurdle once prior to negotiating a coloured obstacle of the handlers choice. This we refer to as the opening sequence. If the first red fence is knocked down the dog does not score and that fence cannot be taken again. The dog must take one of the two remaining red fences having lost the opportunity of an attempt at the first chosen colour. This also applies to the second and third red fences. For instance if all three reds are knocked down then the dog cannot attempt any colours on the opening sequence. The closing sequence is for the dog to tackle the remaining colours in normal snooker order. Yellow-2, Green-3, Brown-4, Blue-5, Pink-6, Black-7. At this part of the game if the dog knocks down a fence or takes the obstacles out of order he ceases to score and leaves the ring. The maximum that can be scored is 51 and to avoid runs off the time is taken for each dog so that the fastest dog with the highest score becomes the winner. It is also necessary to put a maximum time on the course so that the event is kept fast.

MINIS

The small dogs now play their part in Agility. It is usual for mini classes to be restricted to dogs which do not exceed 15″ at the shoulder. The obstacles should be the same as used for the larger dogs. Hurdles, tyres etc., are reduced in height to 15″ and the long jump should not exceed 3′. All other obstacles pose few problems for the minis. A popular class with the public particularly after watching the bigger faster dogs performing. The heights of dogs and obstacles do not always conform from one country to another. The reader is therefore advised to consult the regulations for their own country.

THE JUDGE

Appointing the judge is one of the early decisions to be taken. The club committee would be wise to ensure that they choose an experienced Agility competitor with sufficient understanding of judging techniques. If the prospective judge has had adequate competition experience he is less likely to design a course that is poor from a handling point of view. This does not however ensure that his own positioning and subsequent decisions will be those that are accepted by the majority. In this respect wise is the prospective judge who takes the honour of judging seriously enough to seek guidance. In many countries it is a requirement of the ruling body that the prospective judge must first pass a test.

Once the committee have decided upon a judge it is usual to ascertain that the appointment can be undertaken, then to confirm the offer in writing enclosing a stamped and addressed envelope for a reply of confirmation.

The judge should design the course and needs to know what equipment is available and what class or classes are to be scheduled. This information will enable him to decide the course prior to the event so that it can be speedily built on the day from a sketch of the layout. Needless to say it is necessary for the judge to keep the course details secret until commencing to build on the day, thereby avoiding any suspicion that some competitors have had the chance to practise. A discussion between the judge and the chief steward about possible courses maybe required but this need not have the effect of the judges course plans being disclosed. It is the judges responsibility to determine the course time. The time is very critical and can make a big difference to the result therefore it is discussed in greater detail under judging. Without doubt the two most important tasks to be undertaken is to build the right course and place the right time upon it.

Other small but important points that should be established at the outset are what expenses will be required, and if the judge is to travel any appreciable distance will overnight accommodation be necessary? It must also be established whether the judge will wish to be responsible for the provision of any of the stewards. In this respect the judge may wish to supply a marker steward so that writing will not be a distraction from absolute concentration while the dogs are jumping.

The promoting club must remember that just as the competitors will need directions and passes to the venue so will the judge and steward. A judge who has difficulty finding the venue does not commence his engagement with an impression of good organisation.

OTHER DECISIONS

The question of how many competitive rounds it is possible to achieve in a given time must be considered. While two rounds will often be seen to be completed in one and a half minutes it would be misleading to base time calculations on such speed. Allowing for the time spent entering and leaving the ring it is safe to base the average on 40 dogs an hour. Some will be disqualified thereby not completing the course while other dogs will complete a fast clear round. If eight hours are available with an hours break for lunch then it can be seen that 280 rounds are possible. In a jumping class with an excellent team of stewards I have in fact worked at a rate in excess of 60 per hour. However I would not recommend this as a normal practise for to keep this up all day long requires considerable stamina. That is if the judge is to do his job properly, not just remaining static. However several other factors have to be considered. For example if there are different classes, time has to be allowed for the result to be determined and the prizes awarded. Also if the next class involves course alterations it would be prudent to allow 30 minutes for a major removal and replacement, with 15 minutes allotted for minor alterations. Runs off may be necessary so this factor must have a part in the organiser's timetable.

The club committee should carefully consider the likely overall costs of the event before determining the entry fee. It is possible for costs to be reduced by sponsorship, but it is foolhardy for clubs to schedule an artificially low entry fee to attract entries. Such practises played a part in making Obedience shows grow to unmanageable proportions, with subsequent unpopular legislation becoming necessary. When entry fees are too low, many people will have a go, knowing full well that their dog is not really of a good enough standard to compete at that level. They usually delude themselves that luck may be on their side if all others fail. Of course such luck rarely ever happens.

Running orders are essential for a well organised event. An impartial draw is the fairest way to determine the order, and this is best carried out prior to the day. If there is to be more than one class

then each class should have a separate running order. It should
ensure that no competitor entering several classes is consistently
placed in the same half of the draw. Having been allotted a running
order it must be the handlers responsibility to be available when
required. In the absence of specific rules it is advisable that clubs
adopt the attitude of automatic disqualification if a dog and handler
are not available when required. If only one ring is in operation there
is usually no excuse to be missing. However when more than one ring
is active, with some people handling different dogs in different rings,
some relaxation of the running order becomes inevitable. Dependent
upon the distance between the rings and where the dogs are to be kept
the organisers can request the judges to adopt an agreed system of
controlled relaxation. Such a system has become known as the rule
of five or ten dependent upon distances etc. All this means is that a
handler must report to the collecting ring steward that they will be
unable to be in attendance when their time comes. This claim must be
seen as being genuine and reasonable. If so the stewards should then
tell them they must report back within five to ten dogs of their
original running order. Many good reasons could be advanced as to
why organisors should arrange or alter a draw. Doing so can allow
the show to run smoothly without complaint from competitors.

THE SCHEDULE

When a club decides to promote an Agility event many decisions
have to be taken. Some decisions will need to be announced in the
schedule so that intending competitors are quite clear as to what they
are entering and the rules under which they do so.

The three most important items which should be prominently
displayed are the name of the club, the venue, and date on which the
event will be held. Almost as important is an announcement of the
date upon which entries will close.

The entry fee must be decided and specified in the schedule and
this figure will be arrived at by calculating all expected costs against
an estimated number of entries. This is always difficult on the first
occasion, but following events can be dealt with in the light of
previous experience. Many winter events in Britain are held indoors
at venues that cost more than the usual outdoor sports ground etc.
Inevitably this means a higher entrance fee but promoting clubs
should not be greedy. It has to be remembered that Agility is an
amateur sport.

The classes to be scheduled must be clearly and concisely stated so that intending competitors will have a very good idea of what will be expected of them. In Britain, unlike the early days, many classes are now standard so minimal description is acceptable, but it should always be remembered that there will be handlers entering for the first time. What may be obvious to the seasoned competitor may mean nothing to the newcomer. It is therefore wise for as much detail as possible to be given where space in the schedule permits.

Whilst few competitors are influenced by prize money it is important that matters relating to prize money, or the fact that none is to be awarded, is clearly stated. To receive money is usually a pleasure to most people and sometimes it is offered by sponsors. There are divided opinions as to whether an Agility event should have prize money on offer. In my opinion it is a relatively unimportant issue provided the answer is stated in the schedule.

The person to whom entries are to be sent must be specified on the schedule as should the name in which cheques are to be made payable. Most clubs do not like cheques made payable to an individual so it is wise to specify how cheques are to be completed.

Trophies can be a difficult problem. Certainly it is my experience that this is where the competitors like to see available monies spent. If trophies are only to be held by the winners until the next event, then certain recovery problems can arise. It is quite amazing how difficult it becomes to get trophies returned that are only held from event to event. For this reason I have always felt that except for very big events, it is better to award trophies that competitors may keep. The majority of competitors seem to feel happier with this arrangement for, when winning means keeping the trophy, it is theirs to gloat over long after days of glory have passed.

Certificates are another point that should not be overlooked by clubs. At an Agility Test I was organising in the South of England during 1980 I decided that competitors completing clear rounds should be issued with clear round certificates. They were very much appreciated by competitors particularly those not placed high enough to receive any other award. As entries continue to increase such certificates become more of an attraction as, even when winning is unlikely, the fact that a clear round certificate can be obtained is some incentive to the handler. A good way of organising these awards is for them to be available on the scorers table already signed by the judge. When a dog completes a clear round the certificate can immediately be written and passed to the handler concerned without involving other club officials in time consuming work at the end of the event.

Rosettes are a traditional British award although not all other countries use them. Many handlers prize these momentos and it has become an accepted practise for them to be awarded in order of merit to approximately ten per cent of the entry in a given class.

The judge should design the course whilst also deciding the time that will be placed upon it. The design of the courses are secret until actually built or drawn on paper and displayed just prior to commencement. Once the course has been built, either before or after handlers have walked it, a judges briefing is held to explain a few simple matters about the class and its judging. Such a practise is more necessary for the classes where newcomers to the sport are taking part. In classes just containing the experienced, briefings have to a large extent become unnecessary.

Other imperative announcements that schedules should contain are the time at which judging commences and if possible the order in which classes will be judged. Other details must include what will happen if a competitor misses their turn.

Team events often need detailed descriptions unless they are of the more usually understood events such as the heats for Dog Club teams held annually at Crufts Dog Show.

If required by the regulations of the country where the Agility event is to be held the National rules of that country should be published in the schedule. This is not necessary in Great Britain as long as the schedule states that the event will be held under Kennel Club rules. However it is always prudent to remind prospective competitors of certain rules: –

That puppies under twelve months of age are not eligible, neither are bitches in season.
Dogs must not wear slip chains, collars or leads when under test.
That no practise will be allowed in the ring other than handlers being permitted to walk the course before judging commences.

Any other requirements the organising committee may wish to point out should also be shown. Perhaps one of the more important pieces of information often overlooked is a good map or directions to the venue. Nothing is worse than becoming increasingly frustrated trying to find the way in an area that is unfamiliar to a cars occupants. The aim should be to get everybody to the venue without trouble.

STEWARDS

For a smooth running event it is essential that the promoting club supply a number of stewards. All the following duties will need to be performed by someone, preferably with one duty being allocated per person. Bearing in mind that as the sport becomes popular in any country, more than one ring may be used with each one requiring the following duties to be carried out:

Scribe or Judges Secretary	Time Keeper
Collecting Ring Steward	Score Board Steward
Arena Party	Runner

It may be possible in some instances for one person to carry out two duties but generally speaking, with the exception of the arena party, it is unwise to do so.

The scribe has a very important job for the speed at which a dog completes an Agility round does not allow the judge to remove his eyes from that dog for a split second. Usually being placed in as unobtrusive position as possible, the scribe, equipped with judging pad and pen, should note the judges signals without ever being distracted from watching him. Originally the scribe would follow the judge round while he audibly passed on the faults. For various reasons it has been found to be a better practise for the judge to clearly signal the faults, and without doubt there are great advantages to such a system.

When the scribe remains behind the judge sometimes they get in each others way. It also becomes necessary for the judge to turn his head at times thus taking his eyes off the dog under test. When the faults are signalled from a distance both these problems are resolved, plus spectators and competitors alike can see that the judge has faulted the dog as and when the mistake occurs. This means that when a commentator is used, without pre-judging, a greater amount of information can be given to the watching public. A judge always looks more decisive when signalling, rather than the hurried whisper which can be interpreted as the judge asking for the scribes opinion. Without doubt signalling has become the most popular method to indicate faults.

This does of course mean that the scribe needs to be quick intel-

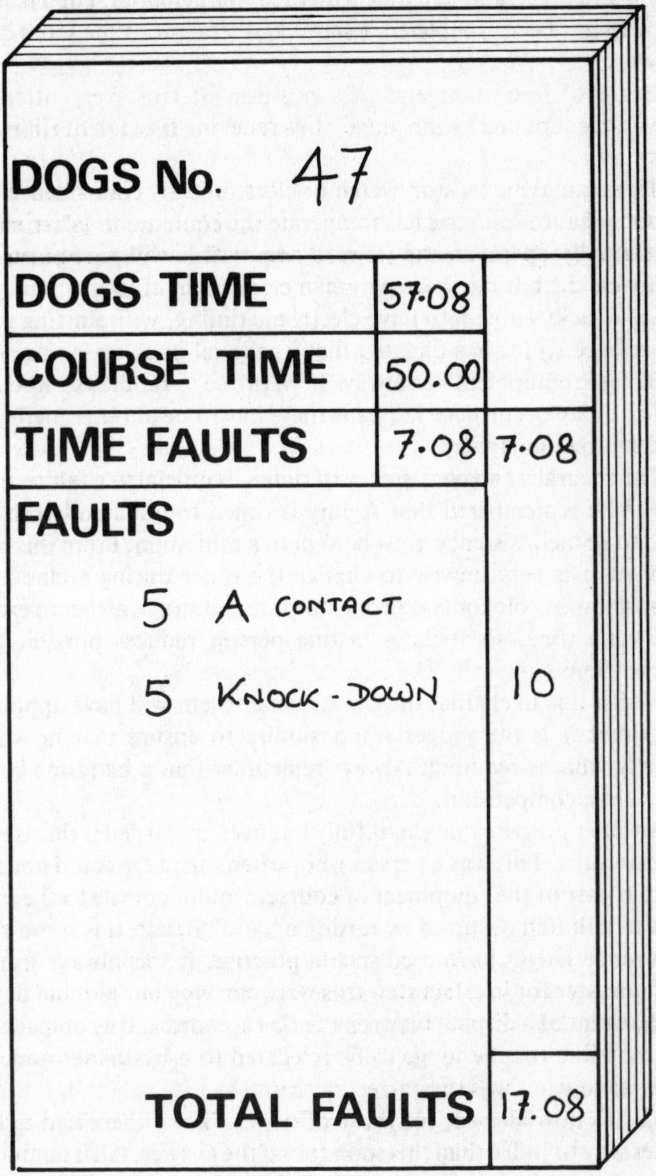

DOGS No.	47	
DOGS TIME	57·08	
COURSE TIME	50.00	
TIME FAULTS	7·08	7·08
FAULTS		
5 A CONTACT		
5 KNOCK-DOWN		10
TOTAL FAULTS		17.08

Fig. 14 Judging pad

ligent and preferably accurate with their mathematics. For as soon as the slip has been completed it should go straight to the score board steward.

Being so important and in a position of trust very often this steward is supplied by the judge, thus relieving the club of filling one position.

Timing may be by stop watch or electronically controlled, but in either instance someone has to operate the equipment. When timing is manually operated, the steward responsible will have to be very quick on the button to keep human error to an absolute minimum. Even if lucky enough to have electronic timing, with starting gates, experience so far has dictated that a manual back up is necessary. Electronic equipment has always been prone to failure, so when this unfortunate occurrence happens there has to be another method of finding the time taken.

The accuracy and consistency of timing is crucial to a fair result. It has to be remembered that Agility is timed to one hundredth of a second so inconsistency must be kept to a minimum. From this point of view it is very unwise to change the timer during a class. It is almost impossible for two people to start and stop watches at exactly the same time, so sticking to one person reduces possible time fluctuations.

Whilst it is likely that the show management will have appointed the timer it is the judges responsibility to ensure that he knows exactly what is required. Always remember that a bad time keeper can ruin a competition.

Another practise that thankfully has been discarded is the use of a flag steward. This was a person who, when the judge could not see a certain part of the equipment or course, would indicate to the judge that a fault had occurred by raising a hand or flag. It is some years now since judges have used such a practise. It was always fraught with disaster for in effect stewards were carrying out judging duties. In the event of a dispute between the flag steward and a competitor it was possible for the judge to be relegated to a bystander none the wiser as to what was the correct decision.

All has now altered, for those of us who knew there had to be a better way to judge than this soon found the answer. All it amounted to was more thoughtful course building by the judge. This aspect being so important will therefore be discussed in more detail in the following chapter.

The collecting ring, as used in Show Jumping, is an essential area which should have a steward officiating. The duties of this steward will be to keep a continuing flow of competitors into the ring thus ensuring that the judging is not interrupted for lack of competitors. It is advisable for this steward to control the draw so that at all times the next three competitors are available and ready to proceed into the ring. Bearing in mind that there may be less than one minute between dogs, this number is negligible. A good collecting ring steward will have this part of the competition under control without any officiousness that might upset the competitors. If the steward has never competed himself he must bear in mind that the competitors he is to marshall could well be suffering from nerves or be keyed up to such an extent that a reaction out of character could easily be provoked. So here we have another essential job that must be carried out firmly, with tact.

The bigger events will usually have a public address system which, if used by an experienced person, can greatly add to spectator interest. Just announcing the name of the handler and dog prior to commencement of their round plus the result after they have completed it is essential in itself. However, a P.A. steward who has experience of the sport and the competitors can greatly enlarge upon the basic details. Of course no announcement should be made that might influence the judges decisions. For example it would be wrong for the P.A. steward to announce a fault before the judge has signified it although it may be obvious to all concerned, but if it is skilfully used P.A. can enhance the competition from a spectators point of view.

The scoreboard steward is essential, not only as an official record keeper but so that each competitor can ascertain the standard the dogs are achieving. If there is a public address system it makes sense for the person using it to be seated next to the scoreboard steward, thus enabling the P.A. steward to keep the public aware of the current leaders.

A good score-board steward will at all times have at their fingertips the current leaders and possible places, so that without delay they can confirm the final result. It is important that the master score board is designed in such a manner to avoid confusion or delay.

This does of course mean that the scribe needs to be quick, intelligent and preferably accurate with their mathematics. For as soon as the slip has been completed it should go straight to the score board steward.

Being so important and in a position of trust very often this steward is supplied by the judge, thus relieving the club of filling one position.

Timing may be by stop watch or electronically controlled, but in either instance someone has to operate the equipment. When timing is manually operated, the steward responsible will have to be very quick on the button to keep human error to an absolute minimum. Even if lucky enough to have electronic timing, with starting gates, experience so far has dictated that a manual back up is necessary. Electronic equipment has always been prone to failure, so when this unfortunate occurrence happens there has to be another method of finding the time taken.

The accuracy and consistency of timing is crucial to a fair result. It has to be remembered that Agility is timed to one hundredth of a second so inconsistency must be kept to a minimum. From this point of view it is very unwise to change the timer during a class. It is almost impossible for two people to start and stop watches at exactly the same time, so sticking to one person reduces possible time fluctuations.

Whilst it is likely that the show management will have appointed the timer it is the judges responsibility to ensure that he knows exactly what is required. Always remember that a bad time keeper can ruin a competition.

Another practise that thankfully has been discarded is the use of a flag steward. This was a person who, when the judge could not see a certain part of the equipment or course, would indicate to the judge that a fault had occurred by raising a hand or flag. It is some years now since judges have used such a practise. It was always fraught with disaster for in effect stewards were carrying out judging duties. In the event of a dispute between the flag steward and a competitor it was possible for the judge to be relegated to a bystander none the wiser as to what was the correct decision.

All has now altered, for those of us who knew there had to be a better way to judge than this soon found the answer. All it amounted to was more thoughtful course building by the judge. This aspect being so important will therefore be discussed in more detail in the following chapter.

The collecting ring, as used in Show Jumping, is an essential area which should have a steward officiating. The duties of this steward will be to keep a continuing flow of competitors into the ring thus ensuring that the judging is not interrupted for lack of competitors. It is advisable for this steward to control the draw so that at all times the next three competitors are available and ready to proceed into the ring. Bearing in mind that there may be less than one minute between dogs, this number is negligible. A good collecting ring steward will have this part of the competition under control without any officiousness that might upset the competitors. If the steward has never competed himself he must bear in mind that the competitors he is to marshall could well be suffering from nerves or be keyed up to such an extent that a reaction out of character could easily be provoked. So here we have another essential job that must be carried out firmly, with tact.

The bigger events will usually have a public address system which, if used by an experienced person, can greatly add to spectator interest. Just announcing the name of the handler and dog prior to commencement of their round plus the result after they have completed it is essential in itself. However, a P.A. steward who has experience of the sport and the competitors can greatly enlarge upon the basic details. Of course no announcement should be made that might influence the judges decisions. For example it would be wrong for the P.A. steward to announce a fault before the judge has signified it although it may be obvious to all concerned, but if it is skilfully used P.A. can enhance the competition from a spectators point of view.

The scoreboard steward is essential, not only as an official record keeper but so that each competitor can ascertain the standard the dogs are achieving. If there is a public address system it makes sense for the person using it to be seated next to the scoreboard steward, thus enabling the P.A. steward to keep the public aware of the current leaders.

A good score-board steward will at all times have at their fingertips the current leaders and possible places, so that without delay they can confirm the final result. It is important that the master score board is designed in such a manner to avoid confusion or delay. For standard Agility or Jumping classes the dogs number is written under the column of the total faults incurred, and in the top of the column on the right is the time taken by the dog. Underneath this are detailed the dogs total faults be they time or course faults. At the top must be noted the course time allotted by the judge for when this is taken into account the dogs course and time faults quickly become apparent. This system means that at all times the result or leading positions are immediately identifiable.

Other score sheets are necessary for Gamblers and Snooker classes. These are called accumulative score sheets. Knockout competitions require a different designed sheet as do team events. All can be found at the end of this chapter.

The score-board steward will need a table and chair, which is best placed adjacent to the competition and collecting rings, so that competitors and ringside stewards are within walking distance should a problem arise. In the absence of an electronic system for passing the judges marks back to the ringside officials it may be advisable to have a person act as a runner.

Finally it is necessary to have an arena party for the erection and knock down of the obstacles. The stewards already mentioned can also help with this duty, and indeed on many occasions this will be the case. However, for the larger event where time may be at a premium it could be wise to have an entirely separate arena party.

The club, in consultation with the judge, should decide whether or not immediate disqualification should be enforced when a dog has had three refusals. On the face of it this decision seems quite simple for Kennel Club rules do state that three refusals disqualify. The only problem is that beginners may be disqualified before they have got very far. To travel a long way, having paid to enter as well, then be disqualified at an early part of the round may seem somewhat harsh. Certainly Kennel Club regulations must be accepted, with disqualification being enforced when appropriate. However the regulations do not state that the competitor must not attempt any more obstacles, so if time permits it could be kind to allow a disqualified dog in a junior class to carry on for a while. Here two points must be stressed. The first being that it would be unwise for the judge to state that competitors may complete their round for a very poor dog could take all day. The second point is that the competitors with experienced dogs should expect to leave the ring immediately the bell or whistle sounds. Declaring a maximum course time covers any dispute over one dog being allowed to stay in the ring longer than another.

As time has progressed all these jobs have been brought to a fine art. Other than the use of computers, which can have entry details fed into them and used to give immediate results to judge and competiton, it is difficult to envisage further improvements. Certainly a computer with a specifically written programme could do all of this plus being able to send the results of each dogs round to a public display. I am already working on this with computer experts but, make no mistake for whilst I would not be without my computer, writing programmes for them is not my forte. With computers being subject to power failures and only being as good as the information fed in it is difficult to see how we can ever do without manual back up, ie pencil and paper.

Finally this chapter is really a list of suggestions and others may be able to improve on those I have put forward. I therefore look forward to a progression of better run events as the sport becomes established.

AGILITY SCORE SHEET – Records Time and Faults – Class OPEN AGILITY Course Time 50 SECONDS

0	0	0	1	2	3	4	5	5	6	7	8	9	
83 43·67 / 0	117 42·61 / 0		91 51·84 / 1·84	70 52·30 / 2·30	84 53·71 / 3·71		45 49·73 / 5·00	52 47·26 / 5·00	85 51·28 / 6·28	44 52·41 / 7·41	86 58·82 / 8·82	72 59·24 / 9·24	Time / Fts
79 41·38 / 0	120 48·32 / 0			60 52·97 / 2·97			42 55·16 / 5·16	48 50·82 / 5·82					T / F
46 50·81 / ·81							67 41·17 / 5·00						T / F
102 47·36 / 0							69 46·88 / 5·00						T / F
104 46·81 / 0													T / F
107 50·82 / ·82													T / F
119 50·01 / ·01													T / E

10	10	11	12	13	14	15	15	16 – 20	16 – 20	Over 20	ELIM	
41 47·81 / 10·00	106 55·16 / 10·16		58 52·89 / 12·89	75 53·23 / 13·23	49 54·92 / 14·92	66 48·01 / 15·00	116 49·11 / 15·00	47 57·08 / 17·08		62 / 63; 80 / 73	127 / 43	T / F
39 46·24 / 10·00	33 48·11 / 10·00			87 53·96 / 13·96	55 59·77 / 14·77	89 55·30 / 15·30		51 53·30 / 18·30		112 / 113; 122	71 / 125	T / F
92 41·88 / 10·00						108 47·06 / 15·00		115 46·17 / 20·00		50 / 114	76 / 123	T / F
101 60·00 / 10·00						37 48·93 / 15·00		62 40·65 / 20·00		74 / 90	124 / 59	T / F
118 49·91 / 10·00						121 60·16 / 15·16		63 60·15 / 20·15		77 / 57	65 / 81	T / F
109						103 47·16 / 15·00				61 / 68		T / F
						108 46·00 / 15·00				82 / 64		T / F

Fig. 15 Agility score sheet

Accumulative Score Sheet

Fig. 16 Accumulative score sheet

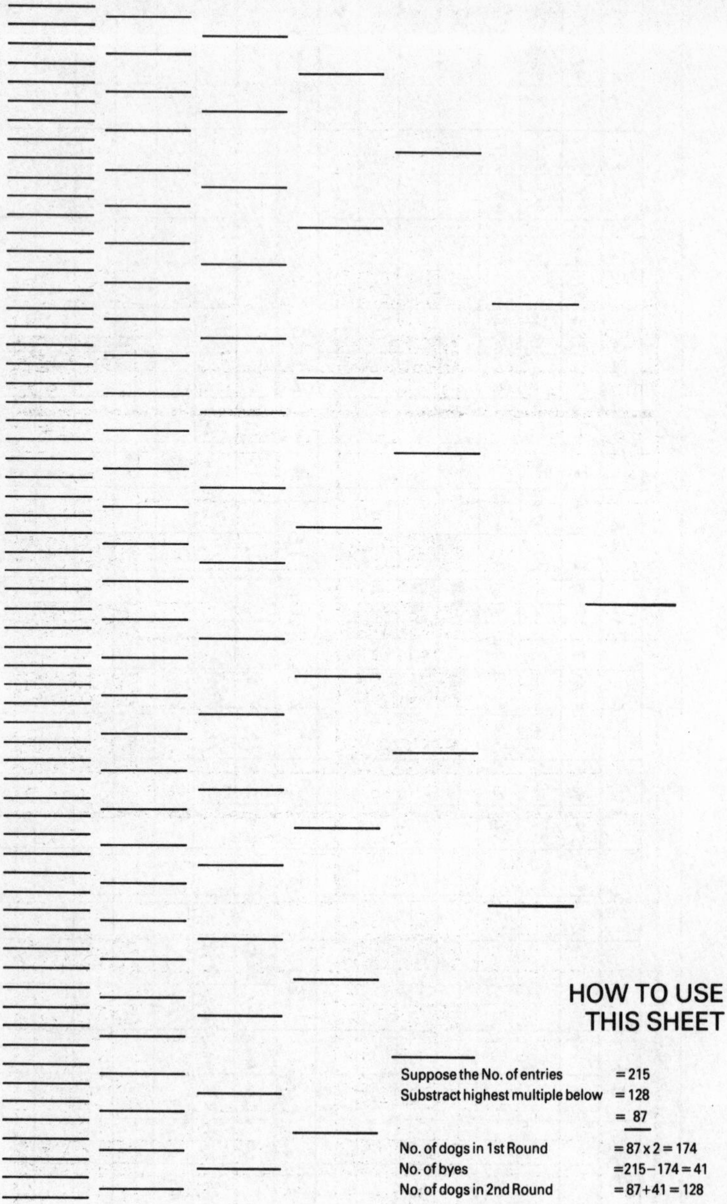
HOW TO USE
THIS SHEET
Suppose the No. of entries = 215
Substract highest multiple below = 128
= 87
No. of dogs in 1st Round = 87 x 2 = 174
No. of byes =215 − 174 = 41
No. of dogs in 2nd Round = 87 + 41 = 128

Fig. 17 Knock-out result sheet

COURSE TIME 50

TEAM 1 — 5th

No.	COURSE F. / TIME F.	TIME
100	1 0 / 2 0 4	5 2 0 4
101	0 / 0	4 8 2 2
102	2 0 / 0	4 7 6 8
103	5 / 8 3 7	5 8 3 7
TOTAL	4 5 4 1	2 0 6 3 1

TEAM 2 — 6th

No.	COURSE F. / TIME F.	TIME
104	1 5 / 0	4 5 4 6
105	0 / 7 8 5	5 7 8 5
106	5 / 0	4 6 3 2
107	2 5 / 5 1 2 9	1 0 1 2 9
TOTAL	1 0 4 1 4	2 5 0 9 2

TEAM 3 — 1st

No.	COURSE F. / TIME F.	TIME
108	0 / 0	4 7 8 9
109	0 / 0	4 5 3 6
110	5 / 0	4 4 7 7
111	0 / 0	4 9 9 9
TOTAL	5 0 0	1 8 8 0 1

TEAM 4 — 4th

No.	COURSE F. / TIME F.	TIME
112	5 / 1 2 2	5 1 2 2
113	1 0 / 4 6 3	5 4 6 3
114	0 / 0 3	5 0 0 3
115	0 / 1 0 1	5 1 0 1
TOTAL	2 1 8 9	2 0 6 8 9

TEAM 5 — 3rd

No.	COURSE F. / TIME F.	TIME
116	0 / 1 3 6	5 1 3 6
117	0 / 0	4 8 7 2
118	0 / 0	4 7 3 9
119	5 / 0	4 7 1 7
TOTAL	6 3 6	1 9 4 6 4

TEAM 6 — 2nd.

No.	COURSE F. / TIME F.	TIME
120	0 / 0	4 9 9 6
121	0 / 0	4 6 3 9
122	0 / 0	4 8 7 2
123	5 / 0	4 9 9 9
TOTAL	5 0 0	1 9 5 0 6

Fig. 18 Team score sheet

9

Judging Agility

All dog competitions controlled by the various kennel clubs or ruling bodies of any country require judges to determine the winners. Dependent upon the type of competition is the degree by which the judges decision is mainly individual opinion or something cut and dried quite evident to all who watch. Showing dogs in the breed ring is a matter of asking the judge for his opinion of the dog placed before him. Of course he must bear in mind the breed standard and conformation of the dog, but other than that it is individual choice that decides. Personal opinion has a lesser part to play when judging dog training sports, for usually they have set tests with recognised faults. In many such competitions it is only the degree of fault that becomes personal opinion, for what one judge may penalise another may not consider markable. The judging of Agility involves a very minimum role for personal opinion, as in most cases it is quite evident when the dog will be faulted. This does not mean that Agility judging is easy. Far from it, for the reverse is the case. When carried out well it certainly looks easy to the untrained eye, but knowledgable people will know just how much thought and care has been necessary to achieve simplicity.

Some countries spell out each and every fault in their rules. This has never been the practise in Great Britain which has the tradition of giving the judge enough rope to hang himself. Certain obvious faults are specified in the rules but beyond that it is a question of how the judge sees the problem, or of accepted practise. The method of judging put forward here is that accepted by the majority of British judges. It is largely the system and method of faulting used by countries practising Agility throughout the World.

When initially approached to judge it is best to ascertain the equipment to be scheduled, for whilst it is unlikely that the judge will wish to design the course at such an early stage, it is important to know what obstacles will be available. If the quality of the club's equipment is already known to the judge then all is well. If, however, it is the first event that they are to hold, certain questions should be asked about the design and stability. If possible the judge, or someone whose judgement he trusts, should inspect the obstacles so that any equipment that is unsuitable can be rectified long before the event. There is little worse than arriving at an event only to find that the equipment is not up to standard when invariably it will be too late to make an appreciable difference to its quality. During the initial discussions it would be prudent for the judge to establish the classes in which he will be expected to officiate. If any appear a little different then full explanations of the rules that are to govern these classes can be ascertained so that there is no embarrassment on the day. It is possible that the judge may not wish to be the deciding official for a class with which he does not agree.

Agility in Great Britain was first given a licensing system and a few rules that came into force in 1980. At this stage judging competitions was still very much a question of trial and error. As time progressed, and thinking people got together to discuss the problems, a system of judging the sport evolved. This system holds good today and is that which the majority of countries throughout the world have followed.

The Agility Club in Great Britain has done much to bring about unification of judging practises which, with no direction elsewhere, was very necessary. No doubt over the years a little fine tuning here and there might be needed, but by and large a pattern has evolved which is accepted by a vast majority of participants in Great Britain and indeed throughout the World.

The sport is broken down into two parts. Agility and Jumping. Agility classes usually contain a minimum of two contact area obstacles and Jumping classes exclude contact area equipment. By the very fact that there are no contacts to be touched by the dog and usually no table, a jumping class will always be faster. A judge must be aware of these basic principles when attempting to determine the time, for identical time on each of these two types of competition will inevitably mean that at least one of the two will be wrong.

Without doubt the two most important judging tasks are to build

Without doubt the two most important judging tasks are to build the right course and set the right course time. It is pointless discussing time until the course has been decided so we will deal with the course first.

COURSE BUILDING

It is accepted practise that an Agility, or for that matter Jumping course, should flow without it being necessary for a good dog to be constantly stopped by the handler. Built into it should be parts where handlers may have to demonstrate their control. To a certain extent these two statements contradict each other and combining both factors is one of the arts of Agility. It is very easy to build a difficult course that will require the handler to use slow heelwork to avoid the dog taking the wrong course. Any fool can do this and on occasions such courses still rear their ugly heads. In the early days of the sport if Agility had gone down such a road never to return I am sure it would be dead now. Courses that require too great a degree of control are boring for dog, handler and spectator alike and, in my opinion, have nothing to do with the sport. Inevitably they come from people ingrained for years in the more serious types of dog training. My answer always is that if the judge requires great degrees of control I suggest they inflict it upon the dog training sports that accept it as the norm. Do not however be misled into thinking that little skill is necessary. The reader that has read each page will know this is not the case, but it does no harm to point it out once again.

Creating a spectacle is also of great importance. To a large extent if the course flows the spectacle will be there. It is wise for the judge to remember that the obstacles should be spread across the normal sized arena rather than leaving large uncovered gaps.

Once entries have closed it may be that the judge has such a full days work that working at the normal speed of forty dogs per hour will not be fast enough. There are certain ways in which time can be saved. For example shortening the course a little or even taking out the table can help. Separating the start and finish allows the next dog to be on the line ready to go as the previous dog finishes, ensuring that while the dog is working his lead is moved to the finish. If it is left on the start line inevitably one handler and dog will interfere with the other. Ensuring that the final judging position is near to ones scribe, who can be positioned close to the timer, will also facilitate time savings. All these points added together will bring about considerable rewards, but if ring party efficiency is maximised as well maybe enough will have been done to get through the entry.

Originally Agility judging was in the hands of not only a judge but also stewards. The stewards were deputed to raise a hand if they saw a fault occur at their part of the course. It did not take long to realise that such a system required too much man power and more importantly was taking major decisions away from the judge. By thoughtful course building these problems have been eliminated by the better judges.

How this is done is to remember to position the prime obstacles in such a way that they can be closely observed by the judge. Such positioning should not require him to run or move in an undignified manner. The prime obstacles are those that the judge will always need to be close to if he is to be sure of observing all mistakes without being masked by the handler. They are:

> The 'A' Ramp
> Dog Walk or Cross Over
> See-Saw
> Weaving Poles
> Table or Pause

Combining these factors with a good course for dog and handler is where a lot of skill lies. It is not easy, requiring much thought, particularly when all five are to be used in the ring. However, if well planned it really does make judging look easy, with few spectators realising how much skill would have been required to achieve such a result.

If the reader refers to figure 18 they will note a course which can justifiably be said to flow and could well be good for dog and handler at a major final. What about the judge though? It really is a terrible course from a judging point of view. From his starting position near the weaving poles he will be forced to break into a brisk trot to arrive at the dog walk at the same time as the dog. The problem is, that no matter how good a judges positioning, the very fast dogs over the dog walk will require quick judges movement. If he is already coming from behind, or even level with the dog, he has little chance of seeing the down side contact when the dog is in that area. Even worse will be the judge who now has no alternative other than to run to the 'A' Ramp. It is possible that if he does not quite get there in time he will see the up side contact but have no chance of seeing the down side. The complication is even greater when he will be forced to run round the tunnel or jump over it. If there is a quick refusal at the tunnel how is the judge to see it? By now, after four or five rounds the judge should be completely out of breath, but his ordeal is far from over. He is going to need to move very fast towards the table to count in an audible fashion. From there he will have to run to the see-saw to be in the correct position for both contacts. At this point he is finished, not just with the dog but probably in every sense of the word.

It goes without saying that all the mistakes made in this drawing are unlikely to be repeated by the same judge in one course. However, I have seen examples which came close to such a disaster. When conducting judging seminars some of the courses presented by the students have closely resembled such numerous judging problems.

Reference to figure 19 shows almost the identical course shape but with four of the prime obstacles moved into acceptable judging positions. The course still remains enjoyable for dog and handler but note how little movement is necessary for the judge.

Examining the course in more detail it can be seen that the judge can have a starting position almost two metres or yards along the side of the dog walk thus helping with the fast dog problem. From such a position he will have been able to see the tunnel entrance of obstacle number three. He can stroll into position to see the weaving poles and gently move to a good 'A' ramp position whilst observing the dog at preceding obstacles. So far, whilst handlers may work on either side of obstacles, it is likely that the majority will have been on opposite sides to the judge making observation even easier. As the judge moves towards the see-saw he can conduct the table count so that when the dog arrives at this last prime obstacle he is in position. Now the judge has but a short distance to his scribe and so does the timer. Whilst by no means ideal, given an efficient ring party, it would be possible for a judge, with such positioning, to handle in excess of four hundred entries in a day. A feat impossible with the other course. It requires far less judges movement for each dog. However, not only is distance going to be a telling factor, so is having to run, which figure 19 shows is unnecessary.

Building the right course is one of the Agility judges most important tasks. It should be planned and drawn on paper some days before the event giving time for further thought or alteration.

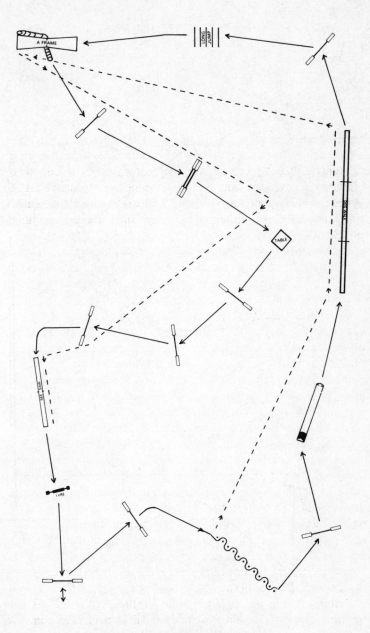

Fig. 19 A difficult course to judge

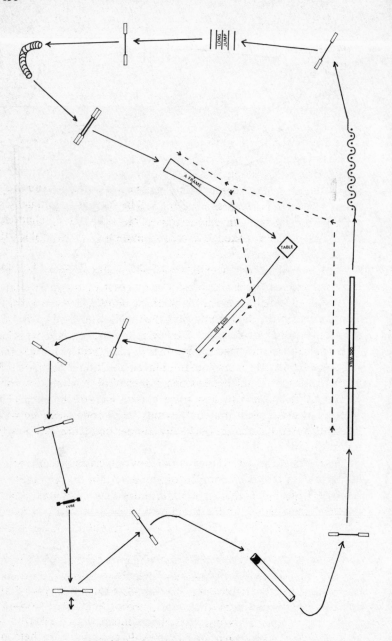

Fig. 20 Judging positions made easy

Wise is the judge who will take several copies of his course to the show. Usually there are a few willing hands ready to assist with its erection and if more than one course plan is available the course is quickly built.

Time can be saved by calling together all building assistants before commencement. Inevitably if not given instructions they will complete building obstacles such as hurdles without realising that the judge may want to move them a little or change angles as the course takes shape.

Once erected the judge should take time to quietly walk round the course, ensuring that it is what he wants. There are many other points to check. For instance, are all heights of obstacles correct? Are both tunnels firmly and safely secured so that dogs do not move them? Is the soft tunnel secured and in such a position that twisting of the material is minimised? It is always a good idea to take into account the wind direction when finally positioning this obstacle. While the ends can be pegged down, a bad angle to the wind usually results in sufficient movement of material to cause dogs to become stuck inside. Has the minimum distance between obstacles been observed? Are the approach angles for the dog right for each obstacle? While there is nothing wrong with some angles into hurdles, dog walks, see-saws, weaving poles etc., there are others where more consideration should be given to the dog. A reasonable approach to the 'A' Ramp allows the dog to have sufficient impetus to climb it. An angled approach to the water or long jump will only ensure that many dogs jump across it. Good judges do not try and catch dogs with such course building. Is the approach to the tyre straight or does the angle only leave an elliptical entrance for the dog? It should go without saying that safety for the dog must always be uppermost in the judges mind and an angled approach to the tyre is putting the dogs safety at risk.

Spread jumps and safety need much thought. When both top poles are at the maximum permitted height, built as two independent wing hurdles placed together, the distance should not exceed two feet (60 centimetres). Without doubt safety is best realised by ensuring a straight approach that allows the dog to have maximum momentum. By only using two poles on each unit, with the bottom pole having one end resting on the ground, safety is again enhanced as poles have less distance to fall. When the bottom end is placed in such a fashion the dog can see the ground line and therefore have a better chance of gauging the leap required.

Finally positioning the numbers must be taken into account. Handlers are likely to approach obstacles from either side so the number cannot just be placed on the left side of each obstacle. Thought should be given to how handlers will pass each obstacle and the numbers positioned accordingly. Another reason why experience as an Agility handler is invaluable.

THE COURSE TIME

The second most important task for an Agility judge is to get the course time right. No easy task I can assure you, and one that not only requires theoretical information but also experience of the type of course that has been built.

Basically there are three ways of tackling the problem. The judge can jog round the course at a speed that he would normally expect his own dog to work. The usual speed of his dog against that which he requires for the competition can then be ascertained. Pacing the course in the knowledge of exactly what ones own normal stride measures is another method. Measuring the course with a surveyors wheel will certainly give an accurate distance, but for this and the previous method, the judge must first of all know the number of yards/metres per second that he wishes to base the course time upon. It will also be necessary to have the ability to accurately adjust this answer in the light of course angles, degrees of difficulty, weather etc. This is where experience plays its part.

Running a non competing dog round the course can give an answer providing the judge knows the speed of that dog in relation to the class to be judged. Also this only works if the dog takes the right course and does not run out or refuse. Running ones own dog round is one of the most accurate ways providing that there is no-one watching, particularly competitors. There is nothing calculated to draw more howls of derision than the Judge and his dog not being able to get round his course without disaster. Apart from this problem usually I am not in favour of these last two methods on the grounds that it does not look very professional in front of onlookers or spectators. The show jumping world does not find it necessary, why should we?

TIME

TIME TABLE

Yards Metres per sec	Course Length	Course Time	Max Time + 50%	Metre	=	Yards
1.75	120	68	100	1.75		2.00
2.00	130	65	100	2.00		2.25
2.25	140	62	95	2.35		2.50
2.50	150	60	90	2.50		2.75
2.75	160	58	85	2.75		3.00
3.00	170	57	85	3.00		3.25
3.25	180	55	80	3.25		3.50
3.50	190	54	80	3.50		3.75
3.75	200	53	80	3.75		4.00
4.00	210	52	78	4.00		4.25

Fig. 21

TIME

READY RECKONER

YARDS – METRES – PER SECOND

	120	130	140	150	160	170	180	190	200	210	220
2.00	60	65	70	75	80	85	90	95	100	105	110
2.25	53	58	62	67	71	76	80	84	89	93	98
2.50	48	52	56	60	64	68	72	76	80	84	88
2.75	43	47	51	55	58	62	65	69	73	76	80
3.00	40	43	47	50	53	57	60	63	67	70	73
3.25	37	40	43	46	49	52	55	58	62	65	68
3.50	34	37	40	43	46	49	51	54	57	60	63
3.75	32	35	37	40	43	45	48	51	53	56	59
4.00	30	33	35	38	40	43	45	48	50	53	55
4.25	28	31	33	35	38	40	42	45	47	49	52
4.50	27	29	31	33	36	38	40	42	44	47	49

Fig. 22

FAULTS AND ELIMINATION

We normally refer to faults in two ways. Standard faults which are all those other than refusals or run-outs, and refusal faults that are as the name implies refusal or run-outs.

The best practise is for the judge to signal faults to his scribe/secretary. In such a way it is clear to spectators and competitors alike that a fault has occurred. It also enables a commentator to do an intelligent job without the suspicion that he is prompting the judge. Many judges have adopted the signalling system of a raised open hand for standard faults and a closed hand for refusal faults. It is of course necessary to differentiate between the two as three refusals result in elimination. Eliminations are usually signified by the judge blowing a whistle, alternatively moving crossed hands in front of the body tell an international story.

ELIMINATION

The following are some of the ways of being eliminated.

THREE REFUSALS

This speaks for itself and does of course include running past the obstacle (run-outs). Such refusals may all be at one obstacle or a total of three over the whole course.

FOULING THE RING

It should go without saying that a handler should ensure that the dog is unlikely to foul the ring by taking usual precautions before competing.

WEARING A COLLAR

Experience has shown, that no matter how safe from unnecessary protrusions the obstacles are, it is added safety for the dog not to wear a collar which could strangle him if caught up.

RUNNING OUT OF THE RING

This applies to the dog that is out of control and for a variety of reasons runs out of the ring ignoring his handlers commands not to do so. It does not apply to the dog that may temporarily duck under the ring ropes while still working because the position of the obstacles make it impossible for him to do otherwise.

HOLDING ANYTHING IN THE HAND

This might be lead, collar, toy, food or anything else that could be construed as an incentive to the dog. The only exception to this would be a relay event where the judge may require the handlers to hold a baton.

WRONG COURSE

This is when the dog takes a route which is other than the judge has designed. It includes back jumping ie., the dog jumping an obstacle in the wrong direction. Wrong course is also declared when the dog makes an initial attempt at the wrong obstacle although not completing it. This could be foot in tunnel then coming out again. Paw on a plank before handler can stop the dog and direct him to the correct obstacle is also wrong course.

The classic wrong course for the inexperienced handler is when the dog runs past a hurdle, and the handler, with careless positioning calls him back so that he jumps back over the obstacle. This also applies to the dog who runs under the tyre who at that point has only refused. If however he returns the same way then it is wrong course and elimination applies.

REFUSAL FAULTS

The dog coming to a standstill directly in front of an obstacle is considered to have refused. Running out, or running under obstacles are also refusals.

STANDARD FAULTS

Unlike show jumping for horses, any part of any obstacle that falls from the position in which it has been set, due to the actions of dog or handler, is considered to be a knock down and therefore five faults.

If the handler deliberately touches the obstacles or the dog it is a standard fault. Accidental touching such as crashing into dog or obstacle is not a fault but the judge must determine whether an accident has genuinely occurred, or has the handler deliberately faked an accident.

Also considered to be a touching fault is the handler who places any part of his body in such a position that invites the dog to touch it. Examples of this are handler too close to the table during the pause so that the dog licks his face, or allowing the dog to run between the handlers legs touching them as he does so. This latter fault usually being associated with the 'A' Ramp and Dog Walk.

FAULTS AT OBSTACLES

'A' Ramp – Dog Walk/Cross Over – See-Saw

Not having any part of any one paw on the contact points of the above obstacles is a standard fault.

Leaving any of the above obstacles before the descent commences is a refusal fault. Descent commences at the apex of the 'A' Ramp, where the down plank attaches to the horizontal plank of the dog walk, and the pivot point on the see-saw.

The See-Saw, being designed to touch the ground at both ends, should carry a standard fault when the dog fails to make it touch the ground. It can be very difficult to be absolutely sure whether or not the dog alighted before it touched the ground so, if in doubt, my advice would be to give the benefit to the dog. The point is that the dog is required to make this obstacle touch the ground more from a safety point of view than any other. Agility never allows the dog to leave an obstacle from anything in excess of a reasonable height. This is a safety feature ensuring that shoulder damage is avoided.

LONG AND WATER JUMPS

To enable the judge to determine whether the dog has jumped the obstacle from front to back four corner poles are erected. They also serve the purpose of position markers should the obstacle require rebuilding. Knocking down one or more units is a standard fault as is knocking down a pole over the brush in front of the water jump. Jumping in from the sides is usually a refusal fault, whilst a correct entrance with a jump out at the sides is five standard faults. Incorrect entrance and exit is of course a refusal.

Having a foot or feet in the water is a standard fault as is foot or feet landing between the long jump planks. However, walking or running through either is a refusal fault.

HOOP OR TYRE

Jumping between the tyre and the frame that supports it is a refusal fault as is running under the tyre.

TUNNELS

If the tunnel is the next obstacle any part of the dog, including one claw of one paw, that touches the tunnels entrance and is subsequently withdrawn, is classed as a refusal. If the tunnel is not the next obstacle and this happens then wrong course applies. Wrong course always means elimination.

TABLE OR PAUSE BOX

When reaching the table the dog is expected to jump on to it and lie down for five seconds. When he does so the count commences. If he moves from the down before 'GO' is called the count does not progress until he is down again. This also applies to the dog that alights from the table during the count.

There are several mistakes the dog can make before getting onto the table. For instance running past the back edge or going under the table is a refusal fault. This means that there are three acceptable sides for the dog to jump on from. If the dog goes under the table, comes out, and then gets on from the side it is still a refusal. If the dog jumps on and off the table it is a standard fault. Should this mean that he subsequently gets on from the back edge it is not considered to be a refusal as he has already attempted the obstacle.

It is very helpful if the judge continues counting the same number all the time he is not satisfied with what the dog is doing. It may be that the dog has risen from the down or has left the table or pause prematurely. Continuing to count a given number signifies to the handler that the judge is not satisfied. There are times when the handler anticipates the word 'GO' a split second before the judge says so. In this case it is preferable for the judge to let the dog and handler continue and signal five faults instead. The alternative is for the judge to call handler and dog back which, if there is a lot of excitement, will result in having to shout in an undignified manner. When a pause box is used which is not often, but of course it does have a use for Mini dog classes, the five second down is still used. The same principles as the table can be used except that the judge must decide if a part of the dog overhanging the box is acceptable.

HURDLES OR SIMILAR

When the dog jumps the wing of a hurdle type obstacle judges declare this to be a refusal. The dog must therefore make another attempt or eventually be eliminated for wrong course.

It is often easy for the dog to run under a hurdle. This is of course another form of refusal but remember if, when he is called back to try again, he runs under in the opposite direction he has taken the wrong course, with the penalty for that demeanour being applied.

It should be obvious that a knock-down of any part of the obstacle means that five standard faults should be applied. The methods of faulting hurdles apply to all such obstacles. For instance Brush Jumps, Walls, Gates, Viaducts, Palisades. No matter what type of hurdle is used, either it should easily fall or there should be a pole across the top that careless dogs will knock down.

WEAVING POLES

This is a difficult obstacle to be precise about. Normally I recommend to countries that are just starting Agility that their dogs should not be penalised for making mistakes at the poles. In Great Britain this was the method by which we dealt with this obstacle during the sports formative years. Being the most difficult one to teach we did not want to discourage handlers from entering their dogs because they had yet to perfect weaving poles. The policy worked, but at all times the dog was required to eventually complete every pole so the penalty was the time wasted doing so. The Weaving Poles are now faulted in Great Britain to a maximum of ten faults. That is five for incorrect entry and a maximum of five for any number of further mistakes. Needless to say the dog must still eventually complete every pole so that time lost doing so is also a penalty.

I do not think we have heard the end of how the Weaving Poles will finally be judged. My advice to the reader is to check the regulations of the country in which you compete.

GENERAL PROBLEMS

STARTS AND RESTARTS

Once the steward or judge has indicated that the dog may start, if he crosses the line before the handler is ready the clock should start as normal and should not be re-started. In other words when starting instructions have been given by the judge, or the timer acting on judges instructions, no re-starts should be allowed.

CEASING TO RUN

No matter what the circumstances a handler should continue to work and run his dog. Only under instructions from the judge should they stop. If the handler ceases to run because of an unusual occurrence the decision for a re-run is being taken by the handler and not the judge.

Excluding the table for a start or finish, the dog should be considered to be in the correct starting position if his feet are on or behind the line. At no time should the position of his head be taken into account.

When finishing, as the first part of the dogs body crosses the line, the clock should be stopped. Under normal circumstances this will be the nose.

NON STANDARD CLASSES

GAMBLERS CLASS

Judging a Gamblers class is not at all easy, so everything should be done to make life less complicated for the judge. With obstacle values at 1, 2 and 3, as described in an earlier chapter, the normal practise is to allow the dogs to negotiate any obstacle a maximum of twice successfully in any direction. It has become an accepted practise to value contact obstacles and weaving poles as 3, tunnels, tyres, spreads and long jumps as 2, with all remaining obstacles, such as hurdle types as 1. The problem is knowing where the dogs are going next and how to be in a good position to judge the prime obstacles. One way is to group the three contacts and weaving poles near to each other. These are the value 3 obstacles and are often the most used, but more important they are the ones the judge will need to be close by. To ensure being able to move into good positions the judge can make the following rule: When a value 3 obstacle has been taken once successfully the dog will not score if the next obstacle taken is also value 3. Such a rule will in effect give the judge a chance to alter his position as the handler is being forced to send the dog to a lesser value piece of equipment away from the position of the prime obstacles.

The judge should always call out 'NO' if a mistake is made on an obstacle. This tells the handler they can have another attempt, for do not forget that two successful attempts is the norm.

The usual time allowed for a Gamblers class is 50 seconds but of course it could be more or less. Very often when the fifty second whistle is blown there will be one or two extra obstacles, maybe with

148

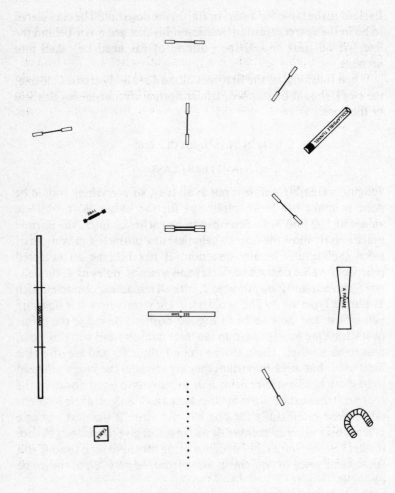

Fig. 23 Gamblers

special rules, which the judge will allow an extra ten seconds for. A typical example of this would be sending the dog over one handle, through a tunnel and over another hurdle back towards the handler. The additional rule would probably be that the handler must not pass the line of the first hurdle. In such a way the judge has required greater degrees of control for what is often described as the Joker which might carry an additional five points. The usual start and finish is on a table. Although a round ends when the final whistle blows, it is normal to expect the dog to go back to the table to obtain a time at this point. In such a way jumps off are unusual, for dogs with the highest score that reach the table in the shortest time are declared winners.

KNOCK-OUT

Over jumping courses Knock-outs are spectacular exciting events but often noisy. There are two accepted methods of arriving at a winner. The first, and the one that I prefer, is least faults wins, but if faults are equal the first back wins. I say the first back because it is normal for the start and finish to be in the same place. The judge will usually employ a reliable steward on each course but will oversee the start and finish whilst also watching the signals from his stewards.

The other method is to employ two judges, one for each course, then add time and faults together. This of course means two timers and two judges who may differ slightly in their interpretation of matters such as refusals. The other possible problem is that while one judge is always the boss, two could argue. Having said all that a major British sponsor of Agility events has run a very successful competition judged in this manner for some years.

With both methods normal judging principles of standard and refusal faults apply.

The judge should always keep Knock-out courses very simple. The pressure of an opponent running at the same time produces many untypical mistakes. For extra excitement a converging start and finish to the two courses can be used, but be warned, one of the toughest tasks there is for a judge is to build two identical parallel courses, let alone two courses that converge and are therefore at an angle.

Whilst not the immediate problem of the judge, if the running order goes astray he must decide what to do. Without very efficient organisation it is possible to happen. It is very easy to have the wrong

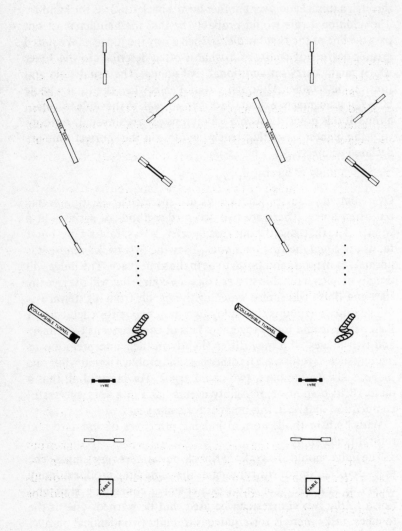

Fig. 24 Knock-out

two dogs running against each other so clubs should not attempt a knockout for a large number of dogs unless they know exactly what they are doing.

SNOOKER

Snooker is a difficult class to explain at the best of times. Refer to the chapter "Organising Agility Events" which gives a description and point values for it is one of the classes where points are gained as opposed to faults being applied. The judge really does need to understand it as do the competitors. In Great Britain it makes a very good class for the experienced handlers but is best left alone where starters are concerned. All normal knock down rules apply but there is no such thing as a refusal.

It is easy for a judge of this class to become confused unless he keeps the system simple and thoroughly understands it. The following is a simple judging system developed over the years by myself and good friend John Gilbert.

Obstacles are set out as in the game of snooker, the only difference being three reds are used instead of fifteen

Opening Sequence: Red – colour, red – colour, red – colour

The three reds are taken one at a time and each RED is followed by a colour of the handlers choice. If a RED jump is knocked down a COLOUR cannot be attempted until a further RED has been jumped successfully. If two REDS are jumped consecutively 2 points will be scored, but obviously it will mean one less COLOUR can be attempted. After a RED, if the colour attempted is not successfully completed it does not score and the dog carries on with the rest of the sequence.

If at any time during the opening sequence an obstacle is taken out of order, eg. (red – colour – colour) (red – "knock-down" – colour) (red – colour then same red again) the judge should blow his whistle to indicate that scoring has ceased and the handler and dog should go straight to the finish line.

CLOSING SEQUENCE (The colours)

Obstacles must be taken in the following order:
YELLOW, GREEN, BROWN, BLUE, PINK, BLACK. If an obstacle is taken out of order, or is knocked down, the judge should blow his whistle to indicate that scoring has ceased and that the

handler and dog should go straight to the finish line.

When the allotted course time has been reached and the whistle blown to indicate dog and handler should go straight to the finish line, as they cross the clock should stop. Placings are decided on "highest score-fastest time" basis.

GENERAL

During the opening sequence only the coloured obstacles should be rebuilt to enable the dog to attempt the closing sequence. A start line or fence can be positioned anywhere on the course, but the finish line should be near the black obstacle. A table is often the best item to use as a finish with either the weaving poles or see-saw being used as a black. The tyre should always be used as the pink obstacle. The benefit of using these obstacles as black and pink is that they are unable to be knocked down, and therefore will cause the judge less problems during the opening sequence.

THE SCORING VALUES ARE:
Red (1) Yellow (2) Green (3) Brown (4) Blue (5) Pink (6) Black (7)

TEAM EVENTS

If the dogs work individually then they are judged in the standard manner. The total faults of each dog (this includes time faults) are added together as is the time for each dog. If there is an equality of faults for two or more teams the fastest total team time takes preference.

When team competitions are run as a relay with baton changes between each handler then individual time faults do not apply. Instead the total course faults & time decide which team wins.

PAIRS AND TWO DOG RELAYS

These classes are usually judged in the same manner as relay team events. A pairs competition is no different; it just consists of a two handler and dog team.

HANDICAP EVENTS

This really is a fun event and as such should be set up so that the faster dogs do have a chance but so do those that are slower. Handicaps are usually by distance. A judge may decide to have three different starting positions according to the way the dogs are graded. He may also require the faster or better dogs to negotiate more obstacles than the others.

TIME GAMBLE

Judged in the standard manner the only difference is that time faults are added for being over or under time. It must be obvious that the judge will need to put a sensible time on the course which as a guide should be average. It is also wise for the judge to impose other restrictions such as no handler or dog should come to a deliberate standstill, neither may handlers look at their watches.

MINI CLASSES

Apart from making sure that all heights of obstacles are correct for this class there are no additional problems. Mini classes usually have standard marking but there is no reason why there should not be Mini gamblers. Mini Knock-out, Mini Time gamble, etc, etc.

10

Agility Around The World

There are always many overseas visitors at Crufts Dog Show and without doubt there have been those who have seen Agility, then returned home and set up something similar. It is therefore somewhat surprising that the sport has not gone in several different directions.

With beauty or breed showing of dogs the basic principles apply throughout the world but rules often differ. In the case of dog training competitions the difference in rules takes on greater proportions so that in some cases the competitions are barely recognisable from one country to another. Of course such competitions usually reflect work that dogs are suited to such as obedience, retrieving, tracking, searching, hunting, security or criminal work. The problem is that across the world there are so many different versions of training competitions that international standardisation has become almost an impossibility.

This state of affairs did not matter so much years ago for most dog people were not great international travellers. Now with the continued advance of the aeroplane as a method of travel for the masses the World has definitely shrunk. It is obvious this method of travel will continue to expand bringing dog enthusiasts across the World into greater contact with each other.

My concern has been that the fragmentation that has happened to other forms of dog training competitions does not happen to Agility. Just for once dogdom has the chance of keeping the rules almost identical from country to country which those of us who really love and care for the sport must try and achieve. What a shame it will be if people with the power to influence rules only look to the immediate requirements of competitors in their own country rather than Internationally. Hopefully this will not occur so that we are able to travel to each others countries not to be amused at the different way the others do it, but rather to be able to spectate in a knowledgeable manner. Thus we can compare standards against like competition in our own countries, converse with each other, language barriers permitting, without great explanations of differences with rules.

Already the Agility people of the world are becoming one big happy family for the sport is not just dog competition it is more a state of mind. Yes there are great degrees of skill required, yes there are good dogs and not so good dogs, yes competition is serious. It is a fun sport, fun for the dogs, handlers, judges and spectators alike with the state of mind being the ablility to have serious competition whilst laughing at the same time. Ours is not a sport for judges with long faces, competitors who do not laugh, and spectators who must be silent.

International competition has already commenced and is surely going to grow. There are of course quarantine problems for some countries with Great Britain being a classic example. Agility enthusiasts in countries that strictly control the entry or re-entry of dogs have an international competitive problem. Who knows what will happen in the future. Maybe medicine will ensure that rabies ceases to be a problem and all can freely move dogs. In the meantime the free movement of judges and teachers is not a problem.

I have been fortunate to be invited to many peoples countries to teach or judge several different types of dog training competitions. In the main it has been Agility for the simple reason that not many countries have Obedience competitions that are the same as that which I understand. Working Trials is another sport that has taken me to other countries, but only a few because the overseas version is usually so different to that which is held in my own country. The ideal world of Agility will allow judges of different nationalities to officiate anywhere in the world without having to spend weeks understanding others interpretation of the rules.

I am certain that by the time Agility reaches its twentieth birthday it will be possible to watch this wonderful game in most countries of the world. In many ways it will be the show case of working dogs, for performed in front of the public they are looking at an ever changing scene. The likelihood of them becoming bored is far less than with all other forms of dog competitions which often require an expert to explain. The concept of Agility requires so little explanation being more visual than complicated. For judges of one country to officiate in another is all part of the visual aspect of Agility and I hope that by international uniformity this will continue to be possible.

The first European country to seek detailed advice from those that really understood Agility was Holland. With several visits from various British competitors and judges they soon had Agility established. Lois Van de Bogarde saw the potential of the sport for her country and had much to do with its establishment.

I remember very well a training trip that four of us made to Holland which could only be described as Agility missionary work. It had been organised by Roger Farr with myself, Angela and Bill Chuter making up the party. We set off from England in a minibus to visit five clubs which geographically would give a good spread across Holland. Towing a full set of equipment behind us the aim was to teach approximately 100 dogs and handlers per club per day. Somehow we managed to achieve the objectives but it was a marathon task in such a short time. We were the only ones who knew how to pack and unpack the equipment. It was all very new to the Dutch people so also its assembly was a matter that only their teachers could deal with. By the time we returned home the word fatigue had a whole new meaning to us, but we had enjoyed ourselves and essentially achieved the objective. Agility had arrived all over Holland.

Belgium had already built obstacles in 1979 but greater interest came later when M. Van Herle of St Hubert, the ruling body of dogs, attended an Agility seminar and liked what she saw. Prior to this I had met Wilfrid Claes at one of the several seminars in Holland where he caught the Agility disease. Subsequently Wilfrid and his wife made several trips to England to study the sport at an event I was organising at Southsea, Portsmouth. It was therefore a great pleasure for me to award a team of which he was a member first prize in jumping and Agility at the very first truly International competition held in Geneva during 1988. At this International dog show teams from Holland, Belgium, Germany, Denmark, France and Switzerland took part in the "best in show ring". They competed as individuals with their results also being assessed on a team basis. I was honoured to be the judge and it was so gratifying to see seven nationalities coming together to pursue a dog sport they believe in.

So Agility had made another great step forward with the advent of International competition. The only disappointing aspect being that the British cannot take part in such events. At the time of writing without doubt British still have a greater number of good dogs than other countries but I just wonder whether in future our isolation will mean others will surpass us. As someone interested in the growth of Agility across the world I would welcome such an occurrence. As an Englishman perhaps I would feel a little sad.

Another country that has made great strides with Agility is Sweden. In 1985 I received a letter from Marie Hansson who within seven days of me receiving the letter was in England to watch an indoor Agility event organised by The Burridge Dog Training Club. This being the club I am involved with I was very busy but asked her if she would like to help in one of the rings and she jumped at the chance. Marie was fascinated and spent 2 days asking me questions before returning to Sweden fired with enthusiasm. With her drive and organising ability she soon called together a seminar during the snowy winter and Agility was on its way in Sweden. Norwegians also attended this event so they became involved as well.

Suddenly at the end of 1987 Finland wanted to know all about this new crazy dog game so it was a case of off to the snowy north again and how rewarding that trip has been. The enthusiasm was so infective that within six months they had produced several good dogs.

Although a small strip of water separates Britain from France it was not until December 1987 that the French really woke up to the potential of Agility. They may have entered the field much later than other European countries but they certainly compensated for that with the explosion of the sport once they had made up their minds to take part. Probably at the time of writing at least 100 clubs have good quality sets of obstacles. This growth and enthusiasm has been due to the very generous sponsorship of their leading dry dog food manufacturer Royal Canin. France has many good working dog handlers so I would expect them to play a major part in Agility's future.

The West Germans, whilst doing a form of regimented Agility that has not surprisingly never really taken off, are now adopting the same system used by others. I am sure that the future will see this country making great strides forward. With Denmark, Switzerland and Spain not being left behind either, we now have a solid block of Agility addicts across Western Europe. Certainly its growth in Europe will continue at a rapid pace.

Agility is not confined to Europe. Many of the English speaking countries in other continents have already established the sport and no doubt as the word spreads it will be difficult to find countries not involved.

The list of countries practising the sport of Agility is probably by no means complete but it is the best information available at the time of going to press:

AUSTRALIA

In September 1986 the Australian Kennel Club recognised Agility. Contact: The Australian National Kennel Council, Royal Showgrounds, Epsom Road, Ascot Vale, Vic. 3036 Australia.

BELGIUM

Holding something in excess of thirty competitions a year Belgium only officially approved Agility in 1987.
Contact: Mme. Van Herle, Kastangedreef 14, 2080 Kapellen.
Contact: Societe Royale Saint-Hubert, Avenue de l'Armee 25, B-1040, Brussels.

BERMUDA

Usually practised just as demonstrations and not yet officially approved Agility has reached this island.
Contact: Mrs Kay Collins, P.O. Box SB 119, Sandys S.B. BX.

CANADA

Agility is not yet officially recognised in this country but they are showing much interest.
Contact: Ian Trott, 3248 Mainsail Crescent, Mississauga, Ontario.
Contact: The Canadian Kennel Club, 2150 Bloor Street West, Toronto, Ontario.

CHANNEL ISLANDS – GUERNSEY & ALDERNEY

1984 was the date when Agility was first approved in Guernsey.
Contact: Mrs Monique De Carteret, Island Dog Training Club, Springfield, Route Militaire, Vale, Guernsey.
Contact: Mrs P. M. Wood, Guernsey Dog Club, Le Hurel Farm, St Saviour's, Guernsey.

CHANNEL ISLANDS – JERSEY

Started competition in 1986. Hold several events a year.
Contact: Mrs Alex Vautier, Karian Dawn, La Grand Rue, St Mary, Jersey.

Contact: Jersey Dog Club, Toneham Lodge, Princes Tower Road, St Saviour, Jersey.

DENMARK

Approved by the Danish Kennel Club in 1988 Agility is likely to grow very fast.

Contact: Hans Ove Pedersen, Norgesvej, 14b, 2800 Lyngby.

Contact: Dansk Kennelclub, Parkvej 1, Jersie Strand, 2680 Solrad Strand.

Contact: Anders Kier, Dansk Agility Forening, Viborgvej 77, 8600 Silkeborg, Denmark.

FINLAND

Having seen what was happening in Sweden with Agility Finland took steps late in 1987 to establish the sport in their own country. Several competitions were held during 1988 and now many clubs are practising the sport.

Contact: Sirpa Pelica, Suomen Kennelliitto-Finska Kennelklubben, Kamreerintie 8, SE 02770. Espoo.

FRANCE

Approved officially by the French Kennel Club (SCC) in 1988 the sport is to be known as Concours d'Agility. The number of clubs taking part will exceed 100 by 1989 with the major event being the annual French Championships.

Contact: Jean-Paul Petitdidier, President Sub Commission for Agility, la Rue de Coussac, 67610, La Wantzenau.

Contact: Societe Centrale Canine, 215 Rue St Denis, 75093 Paris, Cedex 02.

HOLLAND

Known as Behendigheid the Dutch started Agility not long after the British. With approximately 20 events a year the sport is well established.

Contact: Chris De Groot, de Perponcherstraat 70, 2518 SW, Den Haag.

Contact: Raad van Beheer op Kynologisch Gebied in Nederland, Emmalaan 16, Amsterdam.

IRELAND

Commenced competition during 1982 and hold in excess of 20 competitions a year.

Contact: Mr Robert Loftus, Northside Dog Training Club, 2 Glenwood Road, Rahgny, Dublin 5.

Contact: The Irish Kennel Club Ltd., Fottrell House, 23 Earlsfort Terrace, Dublin 2.

NEW ZEALAND

Approved in 1987 many clubs practise Agility.

Contact: NZKC Obedience Chairperson, Mrs R. Cleator, Gladstone Road, RD Levin.

Contact: New Zealand Kennel Club, Private bag, Porirua.

NORWAY

Norway holds many Agility events having started in 1986.

Contact: Jon Olsen, Norsk Kennelklub, Box 163-Bryn 0611, Oslo 6.

SPAIN

On the outskirts of Madrid Spain held its first Agility demonstration in 1987. They are poised to surge ahead although at the time of going to press the sport is not yet officially recognised.

Contact: Carlos Duron, c/Alesandro Moran, 33 PB, 28025, Madrid.

SOUTH AFRICA

Known as Dog Jumping and Agility, The Kennel Union of Southern Africa (KUSA) approved the sport in 1983. Events are held regularly.

Contact: Mr W. Wakfer, Transvaal Provincial Council of KUSA, PO Box 752, Bedford View, 2008, RSA.

Contact: Kennel Union of Southern Africa, PO Box 2659, Cape Town, 8000, RSA.

SWEDEN

Agility commenced during 1985 and was approved in 1987. There are in excess of fifty competitions each year with the Swedish Agility Championships being held in Stockholm during December.

Contact: The Swedish Youth Dog Organisation. ATT Rasmus Palmqust, Box 11121, S-161 11, Bromma.

Contact: Svenska Kennelklubben, Norrbyvagan 30, Box 11043, 161 11, Bromma.

SWITZERLAND

Being bordered by so many other Agility countries it was inevitable that Switzerland should decide to start Agility. Interest had been shown by individuals for some time but from the success of Agility at the 1988 Geneva show it is sure to become a normal event soon.

Contact: Schweizerische Kynolgische Gesellschaft, Falkenplatz 11, 3012 Berne.

USA

Whilst the Americans have had Agility for some years now, being such a large country it is very much fragmented at the moment. The State of Texas has been very active both in the North & South and without doubt growth throughout the whole country will occur. At date of publication the American Kennel Club had not recognised the sport officially but this surely will follow soon.

Contact: The United States Dog Agility Association Inc.

Contact: The American Kennel Club, 51 Madison Avenue, New York, NY10010.

What is extremely interesting is that the Federation Cynologique Internationale (FCI) may shortly make rules for Agility which will go a long way to establishing uniformity. The reader will already have gathered that this is something that I am sure can only be of benefit to Agility. Maybe at the time of reading this book such uniformity will have been established.

Imperial – Metric Conversion

IMPERIAL   METRIC

12″ (inches) = 1′ (foot) = 30.48 centimetres
3′ (feet) = 1   yard = 91.44 centimetres

METRIC   IMPERIAL

1 Metre = 1000 millimetres (mm)   = 39.37″ (inches)
1 Centimetre = 10 millimetres (mm) = .394″ (inch)

Inches = Millimetres	Inches = Millimetres	Inches = Millimetres
.25 = 6.4	17 = 431.8	
.5 = 12.7	18 = 457.2	35 = 889.0
1 = 25.4	19 = 482.6	36 = 914.4
2 = 50.8	20 = 508.0	37 = 939.8
3 = 76.2	21 = 533.4	38 = 965.2
4 = 101.6	22 = 558.8	39 = 990.6
5 = 127.0	23 = 584.2	40 = 1016.0
6 = 152.4	24 = 609.6	41 = 1041.4
7 = 177.8	25 = 635.0	42 = 1066.8
8 = 203.2	26 = 660.4	43 = 1092.2
9 = 228.6	27 = 685.8	44 = 1117.6
10 = 254.0	28 = 711.2	45 = 1143.0
11 = 279.4	29 = 736.6	46 = 1168.4
12 = 304.8	30 = 762.0	47 = 1193.8
13 = 330.2	31 = 787.4	48 = 1219.2
14 = 355.6	32 = 812.8	49 = 1244.6
15 = 381.0	33 = 838.2	50 = 1270.0
16 = 406.4	34 = 863.6	100 = 2540.0

Fig. 25